You Are *enough*

5 Steps to Move from Struggle to Strength

Megan R. Fenyoe, LCSW

Published by Megan R. Fenyoe
(616) 460-4529
Email: megan@missionstrengthsd.com
www.missionstrengthsd.com
Edited by Nitara Lee Osbourne
Cover Design and Images by John Marth Perez, CEO 2P's Photography
Book Design by Tamara Cribley, The Deliberate Page

Printed by Createspace
Manufactured in the United States of America

You Are Enough
Copyright © 2018 by Megan R. Fenyoe

Note: The information presented in this book is for professional, personal, and self-development purposes only. The author is not counseling, acting as a therapist, psychologist, or any mental health physician on the reader's behalf. Reader should consult a licensed mental health physician for mental health diagnosis and solutions. The author is not liable for how readers may choose to use this information.

Fenyoe, Megan R.
You Are Enough: 5 Steps to Move from Struggle to Strength

First Printing 2018.
ISBN 978-1724626080

This book is dedicated to the people in my life who have shown me through acts of unconditional love and acceptance that I am enough.

Praise for You Are Enough:
5 Steps To Move From Struggle To Strength

"Megan courageously shares her story and empowers you to live boldly no matter what struggles you endure. If you are looking for a powerful read that will guide you find fulfillment and put fire in your soul, this book this for you." — Steve Olsher, NY Times bestselling author of *What Is Your WHAT? Discover The ONE Amazing Thing You Were Born To Do* and host of *Reinvention Radio*

"If you feel like something is missing in your life or you just want to feel more excitement in your every day, "You Are Enough" is a must read! No matter what you are holding on to, whether it's fear, insecurity or trauma, Megan will show you how to let it go and confidently pursue your dreams. Megan's 5-step process worked for her, it worked for her clients and it will work for you!" — Loren Lahav, Ceo of Lobella, international speaker, author of *Life Tune Ups*, author of *The Greatest Love*, Co-author *Chicken Soup for the Soul Time to Thrive*, creator of *I am* cards, mom of 3

"The book You Are Enough is the perfect combination of story and realistic 'how-to steps' for me to apply to my own life in order to move forward effectively! Reading about Megan's personal experience gave me insight into her life, and allowed me to reflect on my own. The advice and steps that she provided gave me the confidence to move with applicable and tangible actions to take my career to greater heights." — Nitara Lee Osbourne

Contents

"The lotus is the most beautiful flower, whose petals open one by one. But it will only grow in the mud. In order to grow and gain wisdom, first you must have the mud – the obstacles of life and its suffering. The mud speaks of the common ground that humans share, no matter what our stations in life. Whether we have it all or we have nothing, we are all faced with the same obstacles: sadness, loss, illness, dying and death. If we are to strive as human beings to gain more wisdom, more kindness and more compassion, we must have the intention to grow as a lotus and open each petal one by one."

—Goldie Hawn

Introduction

On January 5, 2017, I had a dream that I clearly remembered once I woke up—a very vivid one. I was standing in a crowd surrounded by hundreds of women in New York City, and there was a lot of... pink. As I now attempt to interpret this part of my subconscious, I believe the pink represented *power*. We were gathered and listening to Sarah Jessica Parker, who in all of her amazing glory, was empowering each and every one of us to live the best life we possibly could as single women. She was telling us to simply ignore the negative connotations that society associates with being single.

One of the things I remember Sarah saying was: "Don't let the opinions of others stop you from being the best *you!*"

Then... bam!

My alarm went off, and I awoke from this confusing, yet inspiring dream.

I am an open book. Always have been. Always will be. I wear my heart on my sleeve, and although I am so excited to share my journey with you, I would be lying if I said I wasn't a bit scared as well. I have shared my story with thousands of people through speaking events and coaching. However, there is something to be said about having my life laid out in ink.

Talk about being *vulnerable*!

Over the last few years, I've really come to understand what the word "vulnerable" truly means for me. To be vulnerable is going outside of my proverbial comfort zone—sharing the struggles and the hardships that I've had in my life. Why? Because what I've learned is that people really resonant with others who are authentic. We all have struggles. We all have hardships. If my story can make a difference

1

in just one person's life, then I say bring it! *Bring* on the uncomfort-able-nerve-racking-butterflies-in-my-stomach type of feelings.

I've had hundreds of different ideas running through my mind over the years of what I wanted my book to be about. I was always unsure of how to make it happen. Then during the early morning hours on January 5, 2017, I had the "pink" dream. This was the dream that ush-ered me outside of my comfort zone. It is where I began to *visualize* the life I truly desired. I believe it was God telling me to take a leap of faith and just begin writing. I did just that, and this is what transpired.

I am a Licensed Clinical Social Worker (LCSW), Transformational Mindset Coach, Professional Speaker Veteran, and owner of Mission Strength. I have been an LCSW since 2008, and I am licensed in both Michigan and California. I worked for 12 years in the child welfare system. In 2012, I accepted a medical commission as a Captain in the Air Force. I provided intense mental health and substance abuse treatment to active duty members, veterans, and their families. I sepa-rated from service in 2014, and began working full time as a substance abuse therapist in a hospital.

Although I am an LCSW and a Transformational Mindset Coach, I also know first hand how difficult it can be when life seems to be crumbling around a person and how negative thoughts can control every area of one's life. I understand how difficult it can be at times just to get out of bed in the morning. Feeling lost, alone, confused, and scared. My personal journey through countless disappointments and defeats began early in childhood, and continued even while writ-ing this book.

In 2016, while working full time in a hospital, I began to feel this nudging in my soul to do something more with my life, but I couldn't figure out what that something was. I was feeling stuck and lost. I began a network marketing business, as well as a private mental health practice—all while working full time at the hospital. I thought that being busy was the nudging feeling, but little did I know, I was running away from the pain and heartache I was enduring.

In 2017, after a year of soul searching and healing, I was able to *finally* put a name to those nudging feelings. I made the decision to take a job transfer, which required me to move from Northern California to San Diego. Again, I thought this was what my heart and soul wanted; yet once I arrived in San Diego, I was feeling even more restless. I quickly learned that what I truly wanted was to get out of my J-O-B and out of the monotonous cycle of a 10-12 hour shift in a hospital. I wanted to *own* my life and my schedule. I wanted to work for myself by changing lives, not by changing the life of the person I was working for. I was tired of making money for the CEOs. *I* wanted to be the CEO—the CEO of *my* life.

The decision was quickly made for me in September 2017 (a few short months after moving to San Diego) when my job status changed involuntarily. I found myself with no job and no more six-figure salary. The stability I had for so many years was just ripped away. I was left with nothing, except for my network marketing business, which I was truly grateful for.

I looked at "losing" as *my* defeat. I've never lost a job until this. I found myself playing the victim role, but now as I sit here and write this book, losing my job was the best thing that could've ever happened to me. I could've easily found another high-paying, stable, and full time job, but instead I took a leap of faith in order to pursue my dreams!

With working in the mental health field for the past 15 years and spending countless years in the health and fitness industry, I decided to integrate my love for both into a new career path, which is how I created Mission Strength. Today, I am not just the CEO of Mission Strength, I'm a Professional Speaker, Author *and* I own a health food franchise!

The nudging feeling I felt for so long was actually "telling" me to leave my job in order to begin making my dreams a reality. Although I was scared to death, I was able to take charge and to begin to "own my life," which catapulted me into entrepreneurship. What I was *not* expecting was to be brought to my knees, yet again, by my ex-husband. Don't worry—you get to read all of the juicy details in the next chapter about that situation.

Has it been easy? No. This is one of the main reasons for writing this book. I had to learn how to acknowledge my negative distortions and negative views on life that were shaping and influencing me for so many years. I had to learn to be honest about my flaws and what areas of my life I allowed myself to remain stuck. Once I went through this journey, I had a new outlook on life. I finally felt *alive*, and I can no longer keep it to myself.

I have learned many health and mindset skills over the past 25 + years (personally and professionally). It was the fact that those skills that ultimately gave me the *courage* and *confidence* to step into my *greatness*, and to finally believe that *I am enough!*

Many people ask me where the name "Mission Strength" comes from, and I love explaining it to them. I am on a *mission* to inspire healthy living (mind/body/soul) around the world and it took *strength* to get me to where I am today!

So What Does it Mean to Be Enough?

I spent time asking this very question of my friends, family, and those on social media. These were just a few of the many responses I received about what it means to them:

"There is nothing I need to do, be, or fix." —Elizabeth

"It means to stop worrying about what other people think and to stay true to myself." —Jacquelyn

"That I don't have to change anything to be worthy of someone/ something. That I don't have to doubt myself and how I am handling life." —Cassie

"God created each human unique and complete to live a life with God's purpose in motion… we as humans think we do not have the capacity to be complete BUT I AM ENOUGH for my purpose! I finally know." —Dorie

"I am enough means to me: I love myself, value myself, and treat myself the way I'd like to be treated." —Dana

I came across this blog post from *The Single Woman* by Mandy Hale when I was in the midst of my life falling apart. I want to share it with you before we begin our journey together. I hope that it inspires you as much as it does me.

A lot of us are at some form of Ground Zero in our lives, myself included. Personally, I'm trying to figure out how I can best add

value to the world and positively impact the lives of others. I thought I knew but with the recent events in my life and I am feeling that nudge of something more. What I do know is that I am no longer satisfied to just live life in my own little bubble, shielded from being hurt again. I want to make a difference in people's lives.

I'm also really, really ready for my "person" to arrive as Meredith and Christina said of one another in Grey's Anatomy. I want that person, the one who will treat me like I deserve to be treated. Who will love me unconditionally through all my faults. Who will be honest and authentic.

So now I want to talk to you in the midst of your Ground Zero... whatever it may be. It doesn't have to be something as monumental as losing a limb or almost losing a family member to be life-altering. Perhaps you're going through a breakup. The person you thought was your forever walked away with no explanation and now you're left picking up the pieces. Perhaps you lost your job and have no idea where next month's rent is coming from. Maybe a lifelong dream of yours has recently been snuffed out, leaving you questioning everything about your path and your purpose.

Here is what I want you to know. It's okay to hurt. It's okay to cry. It's okay to ask questions. To yell and scream and feel and even cuss if you need to. It's okay to be right where you're at, without trying to frantically search for the purpose that will come from your pain or the message that will come from your mess. I'm finding that some pain doesn't serve a purpose. Sometimes pain is just pain... and we can let it be just that.

We can feel it without trying to heal it. We can bring our fist down hard on all the feel-good, sing-song, empty platitudes and send the pieces scattering right along with the shattered pieces of our hearts. WE CAN.

Society has taught us that when we find ourselves at Ground Zero, we have to immediately pull ourselves up by the bootstraps and start searching for the silver lining... but I'm here to tell you: It doesn't have to be that way. Life is hard and we can let it be. We have to let it be. It's the only way to reach a place of acceptance with our new situation, our new set of circumstances, our new LIFE.

Your life will be different... but it will be amazing. Your life WILL be different. Whatever you lost: A person, a love, a job, a limb, a dream, your way... it will be different. There's no minimizing that. But accepting that there's no minimizing that and choosing to keep putting one foot in front of the other anyway... THAT'S when the amazing part is going to kick in. Realizing that the worst has happened, or at least the very bad has happened, and you SURVIVED. You survived and you felt and you lived it and you didn't run from it or try and turn it into some glittery "aha!" moment... BUT YOU ENDURED AND YOU PREVAILED.

How To Use This Book

At this moment you may have hundreds of thoughts swirling in your head. Your pulse and heart beat might be slightly quicker. And why, you may ask? Dare I say, you might be feeling excited because you are beginning to visualize and dream about your future? If so... *yes!* Acknowledge these feelings... it's okay! You deserve to dream big!

At the end of each chapter I pose a question. I strongly encourage you to spend time thinking about that question, and to take the time to write in the space provided about the thoughts and feelings that come up for you. This is part of the process. Take the time to reflect on your life, your thoughts, and your desires. Decide right now if you would like to dedicate a special journal for this journey you are about to embark on, or if you would like to scribble notes in the margins of this book as you read and fill in the exercises at the end of each chapter.

The purpose of this book is to help you: (1) to build confidence, (2) to find clarity in getting what you truly want in life, and (3) to get inspired to take action towards building the life of your dreams!

Whether you are looking to transform your physical health, your career, your relationships, or just finding that one thing that makes you excited to get out of bed each morning, you must understand that your mindset has the greatest impact on your outcomes than any other contributing factors.

If you follow this step-by-step system, you will learn what areas of life matter most to you and which ones might have caused you to be stuck. You will learn how to decide on which direction to move forward in and how "mindset blocks" can prohibit you from achieving the life that you truly want. In short, I provide you a roadmap to understanding how to overcome sabotaging patterns, clear mental blocks, and to create positive strategies and healthier habits. Mind. Body. Soul.

Thank you for taking this journey with me. Thank you for taking time to listen to a story from a woman you have never met. My prayer is that whoever reads this book be inspired and motivated to make that first step in believing that they are *enough*, and to begin to live a life of *passion* and *purpose*.

> *"Let today be the day you love yourself*
> *ENOUGH to no longer just dream of a better*
> *life; let it be the day you act upon it."*

—Steve Maraboli

Journal Page

The reason I entitled this book *You Are Enough* is because over the last year and a half, that quote, "I am enough," has been inspirational and has literally been something that I have said to myself over and over again. These three little words have helped me move through all of my struggles to a place of acceptance. Accepting that my past is just that... *the past*; that where I am today and who I am today is *enough*. These three little words have transformed my mind so much so that I went as far as to get these words tattooed on my collar bone so I am reminded. Every. Single. Day... *I am enough*!

What does "I am enough" mean to you? Take a few minutes to write about it.

_____

_____

_____

_____

_____

_____

_____

_____

_____

_____

_____

_____

_____

_____

_____

_____

My Life With "Mr. N"

*"My last relationship taught me that I needed
to step my self-worth game up."*

—Author unknown

There came a point where I stopped writing this book because I was going through a lot of personal drama, and was definitely not feeling like *I* was enough. I was questioning myself about writing a book covering this particular topic when I felt like a fraud, when I felt so sad, so heartbroken, and devastated. So, I stopped for about a month.

But then... one of my girlfriends Jacquelyn came to the rescue. While visiting from out of town, she dragged my grief-stricken soul out for dinner. In a modestly-crowded restaurant, I found a seat at the bar, and noticed an older gentleman nursing his drink beside me. Poor guy had no idea what he was in for when he asked me how I was doing that night. Yes, I completely... verbally... vomited all over him.

After he picked his jaw up off of the floor from having endured my heartfelt, but very real story about Mr. N, he said to me:

This is the best time to write your book. You are hurt, confused, and lost. You are questioning every decision you have made in the last five years and you are using the tools you have been giving to your clients in order to get back on track. People want to hear your story. Your struggles. Your triumphs.

This is why I decided to include a chapter giving you the backstory of my ex-husband. The man I will call "Mr. N."

I met Mr. N at age 34 when I moved to California and joined the Air Force as an officer. We had a whirlwind of a romance and it progressed very quickly. That was the first red flag, but I was so wrapped up in how much he loved and adored me, that I ignored my intuition and fell deeply in love with him. I was so excited about our future together.

We began dating in October 2012, and were engaged five months later on Valentine's Day 2013. We got married in October of the same year. Our wedding was in Napa, California, and it was to say the least, absolutely perfect. A fairy tale. Even though everything moved so fast with meeting him, the engagement, and exchanging our nuptials all within a year, I just couldn't believe I had finally found the one I would spend the rest of my life with.

I am not implying that meeting someone and getting married within 12 months is a bad thing. However, I ignored so many red flags through our courtship. Red flags I now kick myself for not paying attention to. Through my work in therapy, I came to the realization that Mr. N was a complete "**narcissist**." And on a side note, to answer your questions that are dancing in the back of your mind right now, yes, I am a therapist and yes, I, too, go to therapy. Now back to Mr. N. According to the Merriam-Webster Dictionary, the following is the definition of a narcissist: "an individual showing symptoms of or suffering from *narcissism*: such as an extremely self-centered person who has an exaggerated sense of self-importance."

One moment I think I'm living the life of my dreams. I had fallen in love. I finally found the "one." The *one* person with whom I could enjoy my dream life. Keep in mind, Mr. N was a guy who called every day, sent flowers weekly, planned romantic getaways, and was so thoughtful and understanding about everything. After our first weekend date, he told me he loved me. He came into town just to see me every other weekend, as he was living in Texas at the time. In just a few weeks period of time, we were head over heels in love and I thought, "This must be my soul mate!"

Things were going so well, and this person seemed to be everything I could've ever hoped for. He seemed to know exactly how to make me feel loved and how to fulfill my every need. Life was wonderful. Everything was perfect!

But then the unthinkable happened.

The person who once seemed to adore me began to change. He seemed annoyed, unhappy, and started saying and doing things that made me feel uneasy, criticized, anxious, and confused. I could bring up so many behaviors that I thought was out of character about him at the time, but it actually revealed exactly who he was all along. This is a man who bought one of his girlfriends a car on Valentine's Day a month *before* our divorce was even final. Just three years earlier we had gotten engaged on the same holiday. What happened?

There are many traits to look for when it comes to diagnosing someone as a narcissist. One of these traits is called **Love bombing**. Love bombing is an attempt to influence another person with over-the-top displays of attention and affection. We're not just talking about romantic gestures, like flowers and trips. Love bombing invariably includes lots of romantic conversation, long talks about "our future," and long periods of staring into each other's eyes. It's the combination of words and deeds that makes love bombing so powerful, especially considering today's technology. The ability to call, text, email, or connect on social media 24/7 makes it easier to be in constant contact with the object of one's affection than ever before.

The paradox of love bombing is that people who use it aren't always seeking targets that broadcast insecurity for all to see. On the contrary, the love bomber is also insecure, so to boost their ego, the target must at least seem like a great "catch." Maybe she's the beautiful woman who's lonely because her beauty intimidates people, or he's the guy with the great career whose wife left him for his best friend, or she's the hard-nosed businesswoman who has avoided marriage and motherhood because her childhood was so traumatic.

I fall into the latter category. I have always wanted to get married, but for many years I was so focused on my career because I was so fearful of abandonment. Plus, my trust issues always seemed to get in the way of relationships. Then I met Mr. N, and it completely changed.

Mr. N never controlled me—like telling me I couldn't go out with my friends or wanting to know where I was every minute. He actually encouraged me to spend time with friends, and honestly did not care what I did or who I talked to. This was very confusing for me to understand during my work in therapy. I now realize it was a way of controlling me because I gave him full access to my life because

I actually *wanted* him to care about what I was doing and who I was talking to. He closed me off to his entire life, so I gave him access to mine. This included my phone, computer, friends, you name it… all in the hopes that he would do the same. He never did.

The behavior escalated. I caught Mr. N in hundreds of lies, being disloyal, and having an affair for over 14 months of our 2.5 year marriage. But despite all of the atrocious things he did, it was *me* who was treated like "the enemy." Mr. N refused to be accountable, was not genuinely remorseful, and despite being so caring and concerned for my well-being in the past, at this point in time, he treated me as if I didn't exist.

Over time I began feeling even more bewildered. I began questioning myself and questioning if I was the crazy one. This is called **gaslighting**. Gaslighting is a tactic in which a person, in order to gain power, makes someone question their reality. As I began researching more about narcissism and gaslight, I immediately became overwhelmed with emotions when I was able to confirm that the following statements supports the behavior of who and what a narcissist is, and that Mr. N, indeed, fits the criteria:

1. They tell blatant lies.

2. They deny they ever said something, even though you have proof.

3. They use what is near and dear to you as ammunition.

4. They wear you down over time.

5. Their actions do not match their words.

6. They throw in positive reinforcement to confuse you.

7. They know confusion weakens people.

8. They project.

9. They try to align people against you.

10. They tell you or others that you are crazy.

11. They tell you everyone else is a liar.

This is what I dealt with for the last five years of my life. Mr. N, who used to "adore me like no other," made me begin to believe I was "never good enough." I was blamed for all of the problems in the relationship, no matter how much I tried to explain, prove, fix things, or justify myself.

I can't tell you how many times Mr. N told me how wrong I was, how bad I was, and how it was all my fault. He would tell me if it wasn't for the fact that I had trust issues from my childhood that he wouldn't have had to lie to me. He actually believed that. He said the affair was my fault. If I wouldn't have been dealing with my own anger, he wouldn't have cheated on me. *My* personality flaws. *My* anger issues.

I remember this one time he left on his lunch break. It started off as not being a big deal at all. Very innocent. People run errands on lunch breaks, and even grab a bite to eat as that time is intended for. Nevertheless, I just casually asked him if he had gone out to lunch that day. He said he didn't. Again, no big deal. Later that same day, I found a receipt that made it clear that he had gone to Best Buy. I questioned him about leaving for lunch. He lied about the date stamp on the receipt saying the cash register must have been wrong. Why lie about something so trivial and ridiculous? There were constant instances like this that motivated me to play the role of a private investigator in my own relationship. I started snooping after I caught him in several lies.

He blocked me on Instagram and from our computer a few months into being married, and I never regained access. This reaction was in response to my questioning him about the women on his Instagram and inappropriate private messages he was sending them. He had the nerve to call *me* crazy—when, in fact, I started seeing these patterns and lies with *his* actions and words. I became hypervigilant. He let me know that I couldn't tell him who he could and couldn't be "friends" with. Everything was a lie or some form of manipulation.

He went on about how my issues, past, family, personality, lack of caring, lack of integrity, lack of love, lack of communication, or lack of honesty is the exact reason why he behaved the way he did.

13

He made me out to be the crazy one. He had everyone believing that it was my fault the relationship wasn't working. He convinced our friends and family that I was a liar and a horrible person, and that he was the abused one. The perpetual insults, micro-managing, distrust, put downs, and threats shattered my self-esteem and confidence.

Mr. N filed for divorce in 2014 and pulled the papers 3 different times. He kicked me out of our home on 2 different occasions but would always ask for me back. We tried couples therapy however for the 10 weeks that we went he was still having the affair, which at that time I did not know about. I wanted to make the marriage work despite all the craziness and chaos but he eventually followed through and our divorce was final in 2016. I walked away with nothing but my wedding ring, a ton of debt and a shattered heart.

Mr. N stayed in my life for the next 2 years. He would contact me telling me he missed me, made the wrong decision with divorcing me and even took me on a few dates. However I never went back to our home to visit. He would always come to my place or we would meet in public. I believed everything he said to me and I allowed him to come in and out of my life and control me. I was still fully committed to him even after he divorced me.

Remember how I told you that I was having a nudging feeling to do more with my life? Well part of that nudging feeling was telling me to get away from Mr. N. Eventually, I got the strength to leave the city where we both lived, and I moved to San Diego in 2017. The day I moved he met me for lunch and begged me not to leave. His love bombing gestures and words increased. I couldn't stop myself from going back to him. We talked everyday and he came down to San Diego to see me twice. No one understood. I found myself hiding the times I would talk or see him from my friends. I didn't want the judgment from those I loved

Despite the horrific abuse I dealt with from Mr. N, I stubbornly clung to the dream. I kept praying, fighting for, and clawing away to try to get him to return to being the man I thought I had married. Like a drug addict, I kept seeing him and hid it, even after we were divorced. I lied to the people in my life who I loved. I would stay away, then I would return—over and over again. Always praying that things would be different this time.

Rather than getting better, dramatically and rapidly the punishment and abuse got worse. The worse he treated me, the more horrific and manic my addiction to him became. My shame, hopelessness, and powerlessness spiraled down into a black hole. It became increasingly clear that my dream of having the perfect partner and the perfect life was slipping further away. It was so very difficult to accept that the "love of my life" was now maliciously deceiving, abusing, controlling, and deliberately hurting me.

I constantly asked myself, "How did I go from feeling *so* adored, appreciated, safe, protected, and cherished to feeling absolutely devastated?"

"How could the person who professed to love me with every cell of their being become so cruel, conscienceless, calculating, and vicious?"

"How could he throw me away and choose two other women over his wife... the one person who stood by his side and loved him unconditionally for the last five years?"

Is there anything more painful than being discarded? There isn't. At least I can't imagine anything more painful. When I tapped into my inner being, the messages it received during this time were:

"You're worthless."

"You're not wanted."

And the worst one... "You are not good enough."

My trauma at this point in my life was indescribable. If you are presently reeling in agony as a result of feeling discarded, and feeling stuck, I truly empathize with you. During those moments of struggle and uncertainty, I felt like a small child being deserted by my loved ones. I felt so alone, defenseless, and I felt like I just couldn't go on. I often wondered how I was ever going to feel wonderful and happy again.

You see, Mr. N would always hit me at my lowest point. Just when I started to regain my strength and begin to move on... BAM!

He would reach out to me, pretended to "work on" our relationship—even after our divorce. Be intimate with me. And... BAM! He'd pick fights, all while still "talking" to other girls without me even knowing.

He was there stripping me of my confidence, my mental, emotional, and physical health. He stripped away all belief in myself, which left me convulsing in the gutter while he pranced away with his "goodies," otherwise known as my heart and the things that were closest to me— including my dogs, family, and friends. He was filled with anger and revenge, and he believed that I did not give him what he wanted, so he punished me. He just had to teach me a lesson. He would invite me to things and then if I "misbehaved" he would tell me I wasn't allowed to go with him and worst of all he would send me pictures and texts at the events that I wasn't "allowed" to go too.

As I said earlier, I spent a lot of time researching and learning about narcissism. There were many points during this journey where I cried and thought, "This could not be him! How could I have fallen in love with a narcissist?"

What I discovered is that Mr. N had a very serious issue within his neuropath ways. They were split and fractured from the design of his true self. His inner programs were so corrupted by his false self that he was full of self-loathing. He had to project and target his fractured parts onto people in his life that were closest to him. Unfortunately, I was the bullseye. He aimed his insecurities towards me.

Basically, the people that judge, attack, and criticize the most are deeply unhappy with their own inner being. This is what a narcissist does, but does so to the extreme. That is why Mr. N was never happy. He would idealize me, devalue me, and finally discard me. After some time had passed, he would be back in my life doing exactly the same thing. It was a cycle that continued for years.

Mr. N would discard me like I was garbage in a trash bin, as there was nothing else that he could "gain" from being with me. He emptied me out all the way to absolute nothingness. He would also discard me when a fresher source of "narcissistic supply" came along, which included attention from "beautiful" sources, accolades, resources, contacts, and even sex.

Although I was often treated as discarded waste, I somehow doubled as his security blanket. Mr. N continued to hang on to me despite our marital status and his infidelities. It was like I was shielding him from the abrasive coldness of the world and comforting him as needed.

In 2016, a month before our divorce was final, he met another woman, moved her into our home (I was living by myself at this time) and began creating another life that I literally had no clue about. Remember when I said earlier that after the divorce he would only come to my house or meet me in public? Well this was why. And yes, you've guessed it; she was the same woman who he gave the new wheels to on Cupid's Day 2 years ago. Our divorce was not even final yet! Nevertheless, he kept love bombing me. He would contact me. Buy flowers. Be affectionate. Look into my eyes. And like the perpetually hopeful woman that I was, I would continue to see him and talk to him and literally had no idea he had a second life.

Mr. N continued to tell me that he made the biggest mistake of his life with having an affair and divorcing me. He pleaded that he wanted to make it right with me. But each plea bargain attempt was filled with empty words, as he was living with another girl at the time. Again, at this point, I had no idea that this other woman existed, let alone even knowing her name. She was some faceless "Jane Doe." His actions never backed up his words.

It wasn't until Feb 2018—two years after our divorce—that I learned *everything*. Absolutely everything. When she moved in. How long they had been together. The intimate things he would say to her, which "coincidentally" were the same things he would say to me. And, oh the horrible things he said to her *about* me. Horrible untruths that made it appear that he was being victimized by me.

I was beyond traumatized. I felt empty and damaged. Oftentimes I had no idea how I was going to continue. It is honestly so difficult to accurately describe how this cycle of abuse felt and the destruction it caused me. Finding out about an ex-wife of his that I didn't know about and how he conveniently failed to tell me about beneficiary commitments he had with her. I could not believe what I had become. How did I allow myself to fall into his abuse?

The bandage I had put on my deep wounds from his affair and the divorce was violently ripped off again. There I was holding a bleeding heart and my life in my hands—way beyond what any bandage could contain. I lost property, money, connections, my health, and my self-esteem. Yet, Mr. N held on to me, and I fell for his love bombing ploys. It became painfully obvious that Mr. N, despite pledging his love, would never be accountable and change his behavior.

Mr. N blamed me for contacting the other girl. He blamed me for "outing" him about his double life. He ran to her. Tried to fix things with her. He stopped all communication with me. He never once apologized. The last email I received from him was on February 15, 2018. The email was cruel, blaming, and down-right horrifying! It was something to the effect of, "I never want to see you again. You ruined my life."

It was all downhill from there. I was so confused and hurt.

I realized Mr. N—who I thought *was* my dream come true—*is*, in fact, my worst possible nightmare. I realized that this was the end. There was no going back. This realization made the trauma even more unbearable. My faith in life felt shattered. I wondered how I would ever trust again. I felt more powerless and helpless than I had ever felt before.

I literally was right where I was when I initially learned about his affair three years prior. I found myself having to re-engage in my *5-Step* System that I had developed for my clients. I felt so worthless, uncared for, and *so* not good enough. This is why I made the commitment to continue to write my book, even during one of the most devastating times in my life.

I ruminated over so many self-sabotaging thoughts and questions, such as how would I ever get free from the obsessional thought loop about the utter cruelty, contempt, and trauma I endured? How do I ever regain trust, belief in myself, and self-confidence when it was all taken away from me? How was I going to find closure?

Honestly, I came to a realization that I was never going to get the full closure I truly wanted. I couldn't cognitively get closure from this, which is very normal after what I experienced. This is something that virtually every person who has been through this type of abuse does not fully recover from. My belief in my own humanity was altered in such a way that I danced with evil and it scarred me for life.

Did Mr. N ever apologize? Did Mr. N ever repay the money and property he ripped away from me? Did Mr. N ever go around to his family, friends, and networks, where he smeared my image, to fess up to his lies?

No, of course not.

Has Mr. N been held accountable or been brought to justice? No, and honestly it doesn't matter. I couldn't think my way into closure. If I would have stayed in my head, I know I would be dead right now from the trauma [within] that was eating away at me. I probably would be institutionalized and/or heavily medicated without a doubt.

I used to believe that I could not have closure until he was brought to justice, or at least until he apologized for all the destruction he created in my life. I quickly learned that these things would never get me closure.

My therapist would ask if it would make a difference to me if Mr. N would contact me to apologize. I would have to really think about the question. On the surface, it always felt like something that I would want. But I would constantly remind myself that it truly did not matter because I would have never believed what would have come out of his mouth. Even if he apologized, I would have known that his apology would not have been genuine.

Now I have to admit, there were many times over the course of our relationship that I allowed my anger to overcome me, and I would yell at him. Our fights would be intense and downright dirty. You see, I have always struggled with anger issues due to childhood trauma I endured. I have worked for years learning how to control my anger outbursts, but it was so incredibly difficult to control my anger when the man that I loved—my *husband* lied to me. Cheated. Divorced me. And kept stringing me along for two more years while he chose to fall in love with another woman.

I take full responsibility for my actions. My anger hurt him. I get it. I have acknowledged this. I have even gone so far as to apologize and have asked for forgiveness each time this occurred. But my apologies over the years did not excuse his negative behaviors, actions, and decisions. Mr. N would often use my anger outbursts as the reasons he had an affair, divorced me, and lied to me, but I knew that was just his way of not taking responsibility. If I was such a monster, like he made me out to be, he would have never ever kept me in his life for all of these years.

Strength

We don't always have to be strong to be strong.

Sometimes, our strength is expressed in being vulnerable.

Sometimes, we need to fall apart to regroup and stay on track.

We all have days when we cannot push any harder, cannot hold back self-doubt, cannot stop focusing on fear, cannot be strong.

There are days when we cannot focus on being responsible.

Occasionally, we don't want to get out of our pajamas.

Sometimes, we cry in front of people. We expose our tiredness, irritability, or anger.

Those days are okay. They are just okay.

Part of taking care of ourselves means we give ourselves permission to "fall apart" when needed.

We do not have to be perpetual towers of strength.

We are strong.

We have proven that.

Our strength will continue if we allow ourselves the courage to feel scared, weak, and vulnerable when we need to experience those feelings.

—Author unknown

So what did I do to find closure? I began working my *5-Step* System. During this process I was able to identify and focus on three little words to help me gain closure: Release. Your. Trauma. I had to get the trauma out of my inner being. The trauma that caused me to hurt continuously and kept me stuck was prohibiting me from moving forward. It was stopping my well-being in all areas of life.

I learned that my closure has nothing to do with him. Rather, it has absolutely everything to do with me. I truly believe that whatever unfolds for Mr. N is all in perfect and divine order because he has his own life that has nothing to do with me. What does have *everything* to do with me is *my* life. My unfolding and my inner being.

The only reason I learned how to release the trauma was by being brought to my knees by this abuse with nowhere else to go. The trauma that I held onto for over five years caused my life to be unsettled and unstable. I effectively managed it at times. However, it often resurfaced as depression, anxiety, and insecurities. I had to work hard to soothe it, almost like a colicky baby, but these traumas were always there–crying and whining for attention.

My life was like quicksand. Getting out and falling back in. It was beyond exhausting. The more trauma I accumulated throughout the five years of the relationship with Mr. N, the more I had to fight and work harder to not be engulfed in that quicksand. My entire existence became personal development as a total necessity in order to be sane.

When the last brutal discord occurred between Mr. N and me, I had no more ability to soothe internal trauma. I could no longer manage it. There was nothing more I could do, except to release the trauma. To get rid of the dirty and awful toxicity that was left inside of me. This included going back to therapy. Before, I was trying to heal on my own. This is also the time that I started writing this book. I sold my wedding ring. I started dreaming again. I began taking personal development courses. It was time for me to finally free myself. To begin picking up the pieces and moving forward. There was nothing left for me to do, but to stand back up, take that first step, and to begin my journey from struggle to *strength*!

Once I began re-engaging in the *5-Steps* that moved me from struggle to strength, I was able to find closure. I was released from being an anxious, traumatized, powerless, depressed, PTSD-ridden woman to being an expanded, healthy, and prosperous one.

It may sound like a total fluke to have complete closure after what I went through. Suffering from complete destruction in every part of my life... losing everything I worked so hard to accomplish within 30 + years. Losing the love of my life—my *dream* life! Filing for bankruptcy, all while Mr. N walked away with what had been mine. Nevertheless, I finally got closure. I am *finally* able to say again that I am *enough*. And I 100 % truly believe it!

I no longer judge or blame my former self. I am thankful for the "old" me because "she" brought me to *my* knees to be able to release *my* internal blocks that were not allowing me to live as my true self. I know without this experience with Mr. N this would have never been possible. I would have stayed asleep in quick sand, getting "swallowed" in an attempt to manage the traumas and false beliefs that I had for so many years.

I realized that my greatest disasters, persecutors, haters, and enemies divinely and perfectly played a role in my greatest liberation. This gave me the perfect closure. So many of us, while surviving our wounds and simply living our lives, have yet to awaken to our true power and how amazing life really is meant to be for all of us. The truth is: this agony that you have felt powerless to change, you actually *do* have the power to change the circumstances. Whether it be in a relationship, career, or mindset, the power is within you. I know this because I have seen people who have been so broken and traumatized, who once upon a time believed their life will never get better, completely turn their lives around. I am one of those people. You have to get to a point where you no longer manage your internal traumas. Instead, you need to purposefully release those traumas and mental blocks to finally begin to believe *you are enough*!

If you are at the point where enough is *enough*, I want you to hold my hand and let's begin this journey together. Today is the day you begin moving from struggle to *strength*! I'm going to show you how to: (1) make the changes that are not just going to set you on the path to creating the life you have always dreamed of, but (2), to also uncover the answers as to why your life has not turned out the way you thought it would.

> *"Some of us have been through things so traumatic that the human mind isn't built to handle, but we fight and preserve every single day and night. If that is not strength I don't know what is. You are a survivor and you are more than enough."*
>
> —Author unknown

Journal Page

Where in your life do you feel like you are not enough? Where in your life are you struggling? Take some time to be honest with yourself—even though it may hurt. I promise you that at the end of the book you will be able to look back at what you wrote and have a new understanding of how to turn your struggles into strength.

_____

_____

_____

_____

_____

_____

Step 1: Discovering Your True Self

"And the trouble is, if you don't risk anything, you risk even more."

—Erica Jong

Has low-self-esteem been an issue for you?

1. Are you hungry to have something in your life that you are really good at?

2. Have you felt there is something important missing at your core?

3. Do you feel that your ability to move forward into your future is blocked?

4. Are you stuck in a dead-end job? Feeling like you are wasting your life away in a cubicle behind a stack of papers?

5. Do you feel stuck in a relationship? Not sure if you should stay or go?

A "yes" answer to four or more of these questions reveals that there is a reason why things in your life—good or bad—have happened to you. The reason, even when we can't see it at the time, is this: it makes you stronger. This chapter is where it all begins. I will help you to dive deep into your subconscious mind and to discover your true passion.

I spent some time talking to a variety of people over the course of writing this book. I asked them questions, such as where in life did they feel stuck (or have felt stuck before) and what did they feel was missing from their life. The overall response was interesting, to say the least.

Jessica, a 34 year old pro athlete and personal trainer stated, "I feel stuck in matters of money and health. Seems like there is a ceiling beyond which I cannot get. Stuck under the thumb of 'The Man.' What is missing? The ability to create passion for and about just about anything."

Katrina, a 45 year old successful business coach, answered the question of feeling stuck. "With certain business decisions, not knowing what to do or choose; that used to freeze me from doing anything at all if I was unsure which direction to take or decision to make."

And when Katrina was asked what she felt was missing from her life she stated, "More self-care for my body. I don't take enough time yet for movement."

Sarah, a 36 year old stay-at-home mom stated, "I am missing something. That's for sure, but I can't figure out what it is. I have searched, and just can't put my finger on it, but I know I am stuck and I don't want to feel stuck any more. I want to be excited about something."

The resounding theme I heard when talking to people was lack of excitement, passion, meaning, and time in their life. Many people go through life without ever finding their true passion. They sit in traffic or on the bus each day and try to make ends meet. They work to pay the mortgage and for groceries—not because they are excited about their jobs or because they feel they are making a difference, but rather to meet expectations and obligations. It's admirable to follow through on your responsibilities, but choose to take responsible action with passion and purpose. When you do something you love deeply, chances are you may become motivated and good at what you are doing. You will also be more inclined to make a decent living out of doing what you love.

In this technology-driven 21st century and fast-paced type of life that you are exposed to daily, there are so many things that keep you from discovering your true self. In the process of keeping your head above water, you may forget what it is that makes you tick. You may have made enormous life choices based on what other people thought was best for you. Maybe you just never thought about what you love doing. This chapter can help you to take a closer look at yourself and discover who you truly are.

Life has a way of covering up our true selves. We can become buried under discouragement or past mistakes. There are dreams buried under divorce or under low self-esteem, even though we have all of this wonderful potential on the inside. Just because you might have given up at one point, doesn't mean that your dream is buried forever. The great news is that it's still alive, and it's never too late for you to uncover it.

You don't have to settle for mediocrity. You have not missed your opportunity. You have not had too many bad breaks. You're not lacking. You didn't get short changed. There are seeds of greatness in you right now. Dreams so big that you can't accomplish them on your own.

Just remember, change happens through discovery. Change does not happen through negative self-talk, discouragement, or complaining. The following is a list of complaints human beings are often guilty of using at some point or another:

"I'm never going to meet the right person."
"I've been hurt too many times."
"I'm not going to get that business loan."
"I'm scared to fail."

You're holding onto the wrong things. As long as your heart is holding the hurt and the moments of failure, you're going to stay stuck. If I would've remained in the hurt, agony, and confusion from the last five years, I would've never launched my own coaching business, and I definitely wouldn't have written this book. I had to turn it around and start remembering my dream... and to hold onto that.

Do you find yourself reciting statements similar to the following?
"I'll never be in management."
"I'll never get a promotion in this company. They don't even like me."
"My business will never grow. It's hard to find clients."

In doing so, your dreams will feel like they are being buried even deeper than before. You're *digging* them deeper. Instead, get your shovel and start digging that dream house. Some of you have done this so long, you need a backhoe. You need some heavy equipment. Your dream might be way deep, but you can dig it out. You can bring it back to life if it's dead, or simply resurface it. It starts with your mindset, in what you believe in, and your personal self-talk.

If you continue to say self-sabotaging and self-defeating words about not finding a good partner, not breaking your addiction, not finishing college, or not living in a nice house, then you will live into that reality. Whatever that reality may be for you.

The things that leave us hungry to discover the reason why—they are life-changing events. They teach us something we haven't known, or a gift we've never gotten before, or it creates an opportunity we have never even conceived of. This is how negative change gets transformed into positive change.

Life happens, but instead of holding onto the hurt, the pain, or what didn't work out, the key to reaching your destiny is to begin to discover who you are. Visualize your dreams, your passion, and your purpose. Think about what gets your heart pumping from sheer excitement. If you will do your part… if you will start believing in *you* again… you will find clarity.

Now, don't let circumstances talk you out of it. You may not understand why a business didn't "make it" or why a person walked away. Why did you come down with an illness? Were you doing the right thing? The wrong thing? You know how humans question everything. It's all a part of the process. Every disappointment. Every delay. Every closed door is all part of the process.

People need a foundation of happiness underneath them, and happiness is a choice. People can chose to be miserable or they can chose to be happy. Nearly all of the clients I work with come with specific goals in mind, but they are stuck because of their limiting beliefs and self-sabotaging statements. To be truly happy we need to know who we are—and express that in the world. We need to be authentic. We can chose to be victims of our circumstances or we can be survivors.

We need a sense of mission. We may not know what that mission is, but we can sense a yearning, some passionate conviction, and some vision of living life to the fullest. The reason I went through all of the trials in my life was so that I could find my mission. My passion. My purpose.

Honestly, you are never going to know what your true mission is until you dive deep into discovery. All you can do is make your best guess, throw yourself into it, and see how it feels. If it doesn't feel right, find something else.

I threw myself into entrepreneurship after leaving my full time, high paying mental health therapy job. I took time to work through the process of discovering my true self, which allowed me to visualize a life that I was in full control of, a life where I could achieve the goals I had set out for myself. This is when I completely jumped head first into mindset coaching. I had no idea if I was going to sink or swim. I had no idea what it was going to take to create a successful business from literally the ground up with no business knowledge or skills. I began this journey all while trying to work through the pain I was dealing with Mr. N. Talk about an emotional rollercoaster!

This was what had to be done for me to find my true self. I had to work through the discovery process in order to be able to take that leap of faith. This is exactly what everyone else who's found his or her passion has done as well. They dove straight into discovering who they truly were.

So what does it mean to discover your true self?

Discovering is one of the most powerful tools when it comes to believing you are enough. Discovery to me means to find out... learning from experience... adapting... curiosity... openness... moving forward... growth. I use discovery with a lot of my clients when it comes to how negative thinking can keep us stuck and how to really push passed these negative thoughts through discovery. Without the process of discovery, most cling for years to damaging beliefs that become reasons not to try and to remain right where they are. Discovery is what children do naturally—they explore, find out, and have fun trying new things. Other people who discover are explorers, artists, scientists, detectives, and hopefully you!

The idea is to keep redefining your thoughts, and not settling for what others or the world tells you, or what you experienced in the past. It is a search for new knowledge.

The net result when discovery is done well, is that people find a new outlook and feel more in touch with their inner lives and with the assumptions they make. They can view the world more from the point-of-view of an adult who has choices rather than as powerless victims. This can be truly liberating.

"Staying stuck" is the opposite of discovery. Staying stuck means assuming, avoiding, thinking, hiding, living in the past, and being closed to the world. One of the difficulties for people who are struggling in their lives is staying stuck. For example, if you have been in a difficult relationship for years, you may feel like it's never possible to be with someone who treats you with the utmost respect and love. If you have struggled with depression or anxiety for years without experiencing an improvement, you may not feel like "trying to get better" anymore because you don't feel like it's possible.

This is where discovery is vital. The process of discovery includes noticing your belief. For example: "I believe that I am not good enough."

We refer to thoughts [such as this preceding sentence] that arise in response to particular situations or events as **automatic thoughts**. The term **automatic** is used because these thoughts occur so quickly that they are often not recognized, and more importantly, the significant impact these thoughts have on subsequent emotional and behavioral reactions goes unnoticed. Despite the fact that these thoughts emerge very quickly, they often have profound effects on our mood and can keep us stuck because they offer some sort of evaluation or judgment of our current circumstance.

By continuing to repeat self-defeating and self-sabotaging statements whenever life throws you a curve ball, you will remain stuck. Again, this is where discovery comes into play. You need to create a plan to actually find out if that belief is true. This is called **reality testing**.

The key is to learn to recognize those negative thoughts, test them to see if they are true, and then change the negative thought. If you find that it is not true, change the thought to something positive. Discovery versus staying stuck is a choice we can all make. Often people do not recognize that we can choose to actively "test out" of a belief system. Being true to yourself and being able to enjoy life go hand-in-hand.

Thoughts impact behaviors and behaviors (or lack thereof) impact our thought. The key is to take action—and to *not* wait around and to *not* remain stuck in your negative thinking. Don't just stand there. Do something!

Here's how:

1. Think about something you care about and do something about it. For example, you see a homeless person on the street downtown. You then choose to buy them a lunch.

2. Think about a way you were hurt in your life and do something to help others who have been hurt in the same way. For example, your neighbors didn't welcome you into the neighborhood that you just moved into. This might've made you feel left out and unwelcomed. Invite the neighbors to your home, and show them by example how welcoming you are. Certainly, you will find others who have felt left out and unwelcomed at some point in their lives.

3. The next time you are at a party, spot the loneliest-looking person there, and talk to him or her.

4. Imagine being your partner, family member, or close friend. What do you think he or she needs to be just a little bit happier? Take action and do that.

5. Don't feel sorry for yourself. It may feel that you have a steep mountain ahead of you, but it is the mountain that will build strength within you.

All the good things in life come from people who have a deep conviction that everything that happens and everything they do has meaning. Each time something occurs that is big enough to throw us off course, whether it is good or bad, fertilizes the "self" with new learning that the "self" had somehow always been waiting for. It is through that experience that your new "self" is born.

The loss I experienced from Mr. N gave me a specific strength; it gave me the strength I was needing to take the next step in my life. To take control back. To begin to create a life I deserved. That is why things happen to us sometimes—to give us a special strength that makes a new future possible.

Part of discovering your true self also includes identifying your **values**. Values are a set of underlying principles and qualities that we use to decide what is and isn't important in our life. Examples of values can include God, family, honesty, integrity, kindness, or perseverance. Of course, it's not limited to those, but I wanted to provide you with some ideas to make you think about what's important to you. Knowing your values helps you to understand what drives you, what you enjoy, what inspires you, and what you'd like more of.

Before you can set a goal for your life, it helps to understand your values. Everyone has a different set of values and ways in which they can be carried out. Both values and the way we carry them out can shift and alter over a lifetime. Values are like a compass, giving a general direction, while goals and actions are more like the pathways we take.

Another view of values is the river metaphor. The direction of the river represents our values. Provided that our river is heading in the direction of our values, life can still be fulfilling. The specific course we take is shaped by all those things that life throws at us. Some of us may meander down a creek-bed, while others may meet a larger stream possibly influenced by other people, before returning to the main riverbed and the original direction we had chosen.

By building a life and lifestyle around values, we create a life that is satisfying and meaningful to us. As stated before, values change over time and deepen as you understand yourself better. They are in constant motion.

We also need to be **congruent**. Being congruent is when our thoughts and behaviors align with our values and who we are. Do you know what your top three values are? If not, spend time completing the "Values Exercise" in the Appendix at the end of the book.

When you have an opportunity in your life to make a choice about a goal, relationship, or behavior, it can be difficult to decide what to do. So, before you make a decision, review your top three values and ask yourself:

Does this decision honor my value of _____? (#1 Value)

Does this decision honor my value of _____? (#2 Value)

Does this decision honor my value of _____? (#3 Value)

If the answer is "no," then you will probably not be happy in the long term.

My values have changed over the years and the exercise (located in the Appendix) is something I had to complete when I was going through the Mr. N drama. I realized that this was just another step I needed to complete in order to move from struggle to strength.

My top three values today are integrity, honesty, and authenticity. Once I was able to identify these, I was able to learn how to make choices about goals, actions, and my life based on these three values.

Integrity is a state or condition of being whole, complete, unbroken, and in sound, perfect condition. It means keeping your promises and your agreements to yourself and to others. It means being true to your principles and values. It means honoring your word, and when you do so, you honor yourself. It means taking actions that are consistent with your word. This is what gives you your *power!*

When I heard this while attending a training, it blew me away. At that moment, I realized for the last six years I had not been truly authentic or showed integrity. I was broken because I allowed what happened to me to keep me stuck.

I quickly learned that if I wanted integrity to return to my life, I had to honor my word. My relationship to my word had to be whole and complete. My pathway to integrity was to stay true to my word.

Authenticity is acknowledging the parts of your life where you are inauthentic. What areas of your life have you not been open and honest about? To yourself or to others? What events or experiences have allowed you to stay trapped? Being authentic about areas in your life where you have not been honest with yourself or others will give you possibilities for your life that are *real*.

This is something I learned throughout my healing journey with Mr. N. My thoughts and feelings about myself, and life in general, I allowed to be dictated by him. What happened to me is done, but I had to learn and accept that my negative thoughts, behaviors, and actions regarding his affair, the divorce, and all of his lies, kept what he did to me a current reality in my life. I was using our relationship and the trauma I endured from it to justify everything that went wrong. On the outside it looked like I had it all together, but on the inside I was in such a battle with myself about what true happiness really looked like.

Each time I had the desire to contact Mr. N, I would think about whether contacting him honored my value of integrity or not. It did not. Did getting angry, isolating myself, and staying stuck in my negative mindset honor my value of authenticity? No! I also had to remind myself of my values when it came to taking the leap of faith into entrepreneurship. I would often ask myself if staying in a job where I made good money, but was unhappy and overworked honored my values of integrity, honesty, and authenticity. Absolutely not! I was miserable, and it wasn't until I answered these questions was I able to really begin the process of discovering who I truly was and what I truly wanted in my life. I haven't looked back since.

Once I gave up the story of what happened with Mr. N, I was able to breathe once again. I was able to finally take responsibility for my own life, its outcomes, and my dreams. I stopped living the story and accepted the possibilities of being happy and loving my life again.

As this chapter on discovery comes to a close, I want you to remember that it is up to us whether we welcome the process of discovery and try to understand it. Discovery can feel okay or it might feel scary, risky, or awkward. Don't worry if it doesn't feel good right now; it just matters that you try it. In the long run, you are likely to feel good about what you discover about yourself. If we do this, all of the good things that are possible for us, all of the good things that can come from us, will in fact, appear in our lives.

I asked one of my clients to write about his experience through self-discovery and he shared:

> *What I learned from this process is that by trying to like myself, I act in a more positive fashion. It is hard to do this all the time and makes me feel like being on shaky ground. However, I want to keep discovering more about myself and continue to try to think and feel positively because if I do, I will continue to take care of myself and my needs—I will continue to create a more positive world for myself where I am able to dream. Where I am able to handle and cope with life's ups and downs in an honest, straightforward fashion. Self-discovery was a life changing experience for me. —Joel*

No matter how long it's been, no matter how impossible it looks, I'm asking you to start your journey of discovery. The true mark of a champion is to keep moving forward, even when some dirt gets thrown on your dream. Instead of letting it remain buried, you shake the dirt off and continue to move forward. You keep looking for new opportunities.

That dream is still alive. You may have tried a year ago, five years ago, or forty years ago, but it didn't work out. Go back and try again. This is your time. This is your moment. Your destiny is calling out to you. You can't have a weak and defeated spirit.

Once you are able to change your mindset, identify your values, and learn and apply the necessary skills, you will find your strength. The shifting of your mindset makes it possible for you to choose to be happy—to take a leap of faith and discover your true self.

Now is the time to dream. If something happened to you that was big enough to leave you hungry to understand its meaning, and if you answered "yes" to at least four of the diagnostic questions at the beginning of this chapter, the event(s) *were* big enough to strengthen you in an important way. Now you have the basis for something *big* in your life.

Finding a way to change ourselves or our lives is the point of our struggle to find meaning. If you don't seek from within, you can miss who you were outwardly created to be. You may have been knocked down, but you get back up again. Just because your attempt at success didn't work out before, doesn't mean that your greatness went away. It's still in you. Believe in your greatness.

"Twenty years from now you will be more disappointed by the things that you didn't do than by the ones you did do. So throw off the bowlines. Sail away from the safe harbor. Catch the trade winds in your sails. Explore. Dream. Discover."

—Mark Twain

Journal Page

These are important questions to ask yourself when you want to really understand where you might be stuck in life and to help you find the clarity you are searching for. Most people find it helpful to work through these questions with a coach or an accountability partner.

Self-Discovery Questions:

1. What would I want to experience in life if time and money were not an issue?

    _____

    _____

    _____

2. How do I want to grow?

    _____

    _____

    _____

3. What do I want to contribute to the world?

    _____

    _____

    _____

4. Who am I? Why am I here?

    _____

    _____

    _____

5. Where am I going? How do I want to be remembered when I'm gone?

_____

_____

_____

6. If I achieved all of my life goals, how would I feel? How can I feel that along the way?

_____

_____

_____

7. What is most important in my life? What do I value the most?

_____

_____

_____

8. What brings the most joy and peace in my life?

_____

_____

_____

9. What does a successful life look like for me?

_____

_____

_____

10. What are my top five values?

_____

_____

_____

_____

_____

11. What are my top 10 achievements in life?

_____

_____

_____

_____

_____

_____

_____

_____

_____

_____

Step 2: Visualizing Your Passion and Purpose

"Start over, my darling. Be brave enough to find the life you want and courageous enough to chase it. Then start over and love yourself the way you were always meant to."

—Madalyn Beck

I want you to take a moment of silence and to breathe deeply for 1-2 minutes. Connect with your heart and yourself. Allow yourself to be open to whatever feelings and thoughts that may come up inside of you while you read this next chapter.

Are you ready? Here we go!

Are you worried about things that are only temporary? Letting something steal your joy because you think that's the way it's always going to be? Your dream is not dead. It's just not in season. Your time is coming. The right people, the right breaks, favor, restoration, and vindication. That's what's headed your way.

Perhaps you're on a detour right now—something you don't understand. Don't get discouraged. It's temporary. You're just passing through a part of the process. It's easy to remember the hurt, the disappointment, and the failures of the past. I'm asking you to visualize your passion, your purpose, and your dream.

You may have tried a year ago, five years ago, or forty years ago, and "it" didn't work out. Nobody was there to help you. Go back and try again. This is your time. This is your moment. *Your* destiny is calling out to you.

You need to learn to embrace your uncertainty and accept yourself for where you are in the process. All of your thoughts, feelings, experiences, and results throughout your whole life have led you to believe certain things to be true. With all of this "evidence" backing up your belief, no wonder changing a belief is hard!

If you continue to ignore those nudging feelings, you can miss who you were created to be. You might've been knocked down, but you have to get back up again. Just because it didn't work out doesn't mean that your dream went away. It's still in you.

Before you start to ask the universe for what you want, you first need to become truly aware of yourself and your life purpose. Most people set goals on what society wants from them, and wonder why they don't have the burning desire to fulfill their dreams.

The most important action you can take, is to disconnect from that mindset, and decide what *you* truly want in *your* life. You must decide what your passion is and what experiences you want to have. The key is to feel good in your journey toward fulfilling your goals. The only way to do this is to learn to follow your heart and do the things you love to do.

If you work really hard to achieve your goals, but don't enjoy the journey, you're delaying the essence of life. Committing to your goals doesn't mean you slave away at work that you dislike, leaving you to only celebrate the destination.

A real abiding commitment means that you love what you do each day. You are at least as passionate about the path as you are about the results. If you love the path you're on, your passion motivates you to keep taking the next step. But passion alone isn't enough. Passion requires focused direction, and that direction must come from three other areas: your purpose, your talents, and your needs.

First, **purpose** and passion go hand-in-hand. If you don't know your life purpose, your passion won't be guided by conscience. Many criminals go this route; they are very passionate about certain actions, but those actions aren't motivated by a higher purpose.

When passion and purpose point in the same direction, it means you fall in love with the path of service. You love what you do, and it also contributes positively to the world. A synergy is created, whereby your passion is increased manifold, a natural consequence of doing something you love to do *and* which you know is making a difference.

Secondly, passion must be blended with **talent**. Passion can get you pretty far, but there are plenty of people who are passionate and incompetent, and their passion isn't sufficient to save them. Have you ever known anyone who got really excited about an idea, but couldn't follow through?

The good news is that your talent can be developed. You can educate yourself to learn new knowledge and skills. The ultimate goal here is to discover where your greatest talents lie. What talents, if you were to fully develop them, could be extremely strong for you? You may come up with several answers, but which ones overlap with your passion? When you do what you love to do *and* you become really good at doing it, your passion will increase and your results will be amplified.

Thirdly, passion must be blended with **need**. At the very least, you have to direct your passion in such a way that you'll be able to feed yourself. If you master the blending of passion, purpose, and talent, it will not be too difficult to satisfy your needs... even to achieve financial abundance.

I believe that everyone can find an area where the circles of passion, purpose, talent, and need overlap.

Here's another way of thinking about it:

Need = what you *must* do

Talent = what you *can* do

Passion = what you *love* to do

Purpose = what you *should* do

Many people see these four areas as inherently in conflict. How many times have you heard people spout limiting beliefs such as, "you can't make money (need) doing what you love (passion)?"

Nonsense.

I believe that everyone can find a path on which all four of these areas are in harmony. You can find a way to work from your greatest strengths, doing what you love to do, in the service of purpose, and taking care of all your basic needs, including an achievement of abundance. However, the first step is to simply decide to do it.

Decide that your life is worth enough to you to get all four of these areas working together. You don't have to go broke doing what you love. You don't have to work at a job you hate. You don't have to see meaningful contribution as something out of sync with your everyday reality.

I encourage you to grab a piece of paper, or your journal, and answer the five questions on the next page. Once completed, read on to learn what you need to do next.

Questions to Finding your Passion:

1. **What 5-7 things do you value the most?** When answering this question, think about everything from your most significant relationships to the things you love to learn about, any spiritual commitments, and your major hobbies. As you think about these 5-7 things, note anything you see in common between them.

2. **If nothing changed, what would be your biggest regret?** You don't need to spend a long time ruminating on this question, but the point of it is to tell you what needs to change about the way you're living. Although the response can feel negative at first, it is easy to reframe the answers you get as a positive indicator of your purpose going forward.

3. **What gifts can you give to the world?** Everyone has something substantial and meaningful to offer the world, and in many cases, the gifts that you can give are intimately connected to your life's purpose. Come up with as many as you can, considering what friends, colleagues, and family members have noted about the ways you change their lives.

4. **If you could be anyone, who would you be?** This is not an exercise in comparing your weaknesses with someone else's strengths or pretending to be someone you're not. This is about evolving into a stronger version of yourself. Look at the characteristics in others that you admire. Don't restrict your imagination here. Just tune into who and what you would truly want to be, regardless of how different they are from you. This is a great way to realize new things about the kind of person you want to become, removing the defensive barriers that are normally in place when you think about this.

5. **What are your happiest memories?** When you think about your life so far, the events and experiences that stand out are often the ones most strongly tied to your major passions. Once again, you're looking for common denominators in these memories.

Try to see what your answers to the preceding questions can tell you about the things you're good at, what excites you, what you could live without, and how you're uniquely positioned to change the world. Then, ask yourself this final question: what jobs, hobbies, or lifestyle choices could allow you to live in concert with these key values and positive feelings? Perhaps you are already thinking of ways you can bring some of these ideas into your life. Now is the time to begin creating the life you have always dreamed of!

Manifesting the Life you Truly Desire

You have the power to change the lens with which you view your experience and your reality, and in doing so, will dramatically affect your potential for creating and manifesting those things that your soul desires.

In the book *Manifest Moment To Moment*, authors Tejpal and Dr. Carrol McLaughlin offer eight principles that will help to realize the extraordinary power you have to manifest. These principles work equally well in your personal life and in the corporate world, whether you are a business executive, an entrepreneur, or managing a household. The principles from Tejpal and Dr. Carrol McLaughlin's book are outlined below:

1. *You Have a Unique Soul Mission. What is your essence? What lies at the very core of your being? How can your limitations serve you? By examining these questions, you can identify your gifts and what we call the "joy factor" that brings light to your soul. As your fears begin to fade, you start to manifest moment to moment that which you truly desire.*

2. *It's All About Energy. The power of your vibration affects every part of your life and energy flows through you in multiple*

dimensions. Can you understand yourself as a complex unity of all these aspects, vibrating in harmony? When you develop the ability to work in harmony with all the forces available to you, you're able to materialize on the physical plane anything you wish.

3. *Intuition Is the Magic Wand. How do you know what you know? If you use just your logical mind, then you are limiting your knowledge. Go beyond your linear understanding and discover seven elements to expand your intuitive self. The more you trust your intuition, the faster you can assess a situation and experience the natural flow of manifestation.*

4. *Your Belief and Your Story Do Not Define You and Can Be Changed. What is your story? How do you tell the narrative of your life, and what beliefs have grown out of your experience? These stories and beliefs are merely your mind's interpretation. They can also prevent you from being in the moment and taking action. As you change your story, you change your life.*

5. *Your Desire Forms the Basis of Every Manifestation. Is there an outcome you long for and yet somehow never experience? By examining your desire in every dimension, you can discover what may be blocking the manifestation of your dreams. If your desire is in alignment with your essence, you need not be concerned with the "how to"—your desire will be manifested.*

6. *Intention Overcomes Every Obstacle. Intention is an extremely powerful tool. Neither logic nor life's circumstances will stand in its way. No matter what your material resources or station in life, your intention—when clear and focused and sustained—will ensure the manifestation of your soul's mission.*

7. *You Have the Power to Clear, Heal, and Reinvent Constantly. When you carry unnecessary baggage in your life, such as clutter in your space or mental worries, your life force becomes drained. What are you holding on to that is preventing you from manifesting what you want? This clutter must be cleared*

for you to be able to focus on your intent and achieve what you desire. Clearing the energy of the chakras will enhance your vitality and magnify your ability to create the life you want.

8. *Your Inner Guidance Knows the Path to Creating Life Balance. Where do you find the answer to the continuing challenges life presents? How do you choose among the array of opportunities that will grow as you begin to manifest your destiny moment to moment? Accessing your chakras and the five elements will help you find the answers within yourself.*

These principles are so incredibly powerful and are great tools when it comes to manifesting the life you truly desire. It is also important to remember that you first need to *become* the life you want. This means that you need to first change your mindset and your vibration. When you do this, you don't even need to waste your time "manifesting" anything. You can use manifestation to attract things into your life. You can start by aligning yourself with your soul. This means that you need to get in touch with the essence of who you are and go into higher realms of consciousness. You need to become authentic. Through becoming *you*, everything that you need will automatically be manifested in your life.

When you start operating your life from the place of your soul, you enter into this new realm of understanding that everything that needs to come your way will come your way. This includes money, relationships, a job, and so on. So, when you are in the flow of your life and connected to your soul, there really isn't a need for you to spend time visualizing or manifesting anything.

You get to this place through:

1. Believing in yourself.

2. Believing in a higher power.

3. Raising your vibration.

4. Meditation.

5. Working with accountability partners.

Visualizing and Creating your Vision Statement

So many people struggle with taking control of their minds and seeing all of the true beauty that life has to offer because of a lack of **vision**. It's important that we create a grand vision for our lives because that's what pushes us forward, despite whatever hardship or negative situation may be present at the moment.

Oprah Winfrey said it best: "Create the highest, grandest vision for your life, because you become what you believe."

If you can't see it for yourself, then it will never happen. You must be able to see yourself victorious. You must be able to see yourself building a remarkable and dominant organization. You must be able to see yourself get out of debt and become financially independent. If you can't see it, you'll never achieve it.

Creative visualization is a powerful way of using mindfulness techniques to help you to attract success in all walks of life. While these are general creative visualization exercises that can be used to picture and promote almost any kind of goal, you may be more successful if you targeted exercises that are designed to help you meet specific goals.

If you want to practice or experiment with visualization, here is how to start:

1. Think about what you want to manifest in your life, and write it down in just one sentence. Visualize yourself receiving whatever it is that you want. Allow yourself to visualize every detail and get clear with it. Pay attention to how "the having" of this thing makes you feel.

2. Once you have identified how "the having" of this thing makes you feel, start creating this "feeling place" for yourself immediately. For example, if you visualized money because you want freedom or security, start finding ways to feel secure and free right now.

3. Keep your attention focused on that "feeling place," and release and surrender to the Universe. Trust that your

message has been delivered, and that what you want is already there. You just need to open to it.

Below, and on the following pages, are seven effective types of creative visualization exercises that will help you find health, love, and success.

Creative Visualization Exercise—Vision Statement

Describe why you enjoy life and how you believe your future attitude, self-confidence, and mindset will be. Here are some questions to ask yourself:

What are 10 things that you most enjoy doing? These are the 10 things that, if you didn't do them, your weeks, months, and years would feel incomplete. Make a list.

1. **Write one important goal for each of the following facets of your life:** physical, spiritual, work/career, family, social relationships, financial security, mental improvement, and fun. Set goals that are grounded in reality, but cause you to push yourself beyond your comfort level in order to achieve them.

2. **If you never had to work another day in your life, how would you spend your time?** Do not limit yourself here. This is the moment you're able to write what you really want—not what you have to settle for.

Once you have thoughtfully prepared answers to the three questions listed above, you are ready to craft what is known as a personal **vision statement**.

A vision statement is the first step in focusing your life. It can help put things into perspective—your joy, your accomplishments, your contribution to the world, your glory, and your legacy. Think about what kind of career and what kind of life would allow you to put these five areas in harmony—all of them pointing in the same direction. Think "big" and do not limit yourself. Remember that anything is possible!

In order to write your vision statement, you need to write in first person, present tense, and make the statement about the future you hope to achieve. Make a clear story of your desired life with full details using all senses (sight, touch, hearing, smell and taste). Here is an example: I am a full time actress positively impacting the lives of millions of women across the world.

Write the statement as if you are already making it happen in your life. Some experts recommend 50 words or less, but forget word counts. Fully articulate the vision that *you* want for *your* life and *your* future. The more detailed you make your image, the better you can see it in your mind's eye.

According to Motivational Speaker and Writer Brian Tracy, you generally accomplish your written goals, dreams, plans, and visions. Writing down goals lends power and commitment to their accomplishment.

Keep in mind that your personal vision statement can also change over time, depending on what is happening in your life. You might be amazed at how many components remain consistent over time. When people live and experience the components of their personal vision frequently, they can feel inner peace and joy that knows no bounds. Your personal vision statement can have the same impact for you.

Journal Page

Use this space to write and/or refine your vision statement. Read the statement out loud twice a day—once in the morning and again at night before you go to sleep. Whether it's a daily mantra or a quote to return to when times get tough, having a personal vision statement brings focus and purpose to your life.

_____

_____

_____

_____

_____

_____

_____

_____

_____

_____

_____

_____

_____

_____

_____

_____

_____

_____

_____

_____

_____

Need more? Here are the remaining techniques and exercises to practice when it comes to visualization.

Creative Visualization Exercise—Attracting Career Success

Find a space to relax. Slowly enter a focused and meditative state. While meditating, find one vivid image that represents your idea of career success. It might be hearing applause after a great speech, the moment you receive a major promotion, or the way your loved ones react when you tell them that you have achieved your goals at work.

Experiment with multiple images. You then want to focus on one that really speaks to the feelings of pride, happiness, and accomplishment that you associate with career success. This will be the image that you use in subsequent visualizations. You may find it especially useful to use creative visualization each morning before you leave the house, as this process will allow you to carry your positive images, emotions, and beliefs into the workplace.

Creative Visualization Exercise—Improving Health

Creative visualization is *not* a substitute for appropriate medical treatment, fitness training, or a healthy diet. However, there is overwhelming evidence that creative visualization can help to improve your well-being if it is combined with practical strategies.

While part of the success of these exercises perhaps owes to an increase in motivation, certain aspects of the power of creative visualization remain mysterious in spite of its effectiveness.

If you are struggling with a chronic illness, one visualization technique involves focusing on a visual representation of triumphing over your condition. You can be as creative as you like.

Some people imagine toxins or unhealthy cells being sucked out of the body, while others picture themselves being submerged in a healing white light. Feel free to experiment with different healing images until you find out what imbues you with a visceral sense of power.

Creative Visualization Exercise—Enhancing Physical Performance

Athletes are some of the most ardent advocates of creative visualization exercises, often using these techniques to improve their performance. Indeed, one study on creative visualization in sports revealed that Olympic athletes who received 50% physical training and 50% mental training performed better than the athletes who received only physical training or only mental training.

On the basis of such studies (and huge amounts of anecdotal evidence), many neuroscientists and sports psychologists believe that you can actually change and improve your muscle memory by repeatedly picturing successful physical performance.

Once you have entered a meditative state, think of your performance goals. You might imagine the perfect golf swing, a wonderful piano recital, your fastest swimming record, or a flawless dance routine.

As with all visualizations, the trick is to imagine every little sight, sound, and feeling of your ideal experience. Repeat this exercise as often as you can to help you begin to see improvements in your physical performance.

Creative Visualization Exercise—Finding a Romantic Relationship

If you're single and looking for love, you may be your own worst enemy. Do you dwell on your past dating struggles or find yourself constantly worrying that you'll never find someone suitable? If this description sounds familiar, you would benefit from trying creative visualization exercises that focus on love.

One easy exercise involves picturing the perfect date. Each time you do the exercise, imagine having fun, feeling strong romantic chemistry, and presenting the best version of yourself. Alternatively, you might opt for a more abstract exercise that involves filling yourself with optimism and self-confidence. For example, you might imagine a particular object that represents success in love. You would then mentally "hold" the object during your visualization. You may find it most effective to use both exercises. First, imagine yourself being filled with positive romantic energy; secondly, you conjure up a vivid experience of the ideal date.

Creative Visualization Exercise—Developing a Happier Outlook

While there are many ways to increase your optimism, creative visualization can be a particularly useful method. If you struggle to see the good in life or to focus on the positive, there are a few exercises you can try.

One approach would be to imagine yourself verbally and emphatically offering thanks for five things you appreciate the most. Common examples include your family, a journey to a favorite place, the wisdom of a close friend, a pet, your health, and the fact you don't live in abject poverty.

Another approach involves creating the happiest place you can imagine and visualizing that place on a daily basis. It can be somewhere you have been or an imaginary location that represents pure joy. Anyone or anything that you love can be present in this place, and you should spend at least ten minutes simply soaking up the positive, invigorating atmosphere that you create.

Creative Visualization Exercise—Create a Trigger Card

Take a note card and write down your two most important goals in the past tense as if you have already accomplished them.

A while back, I ran across a story about Jim Carrey, the famous comedic actor. In a blog post in Neatorama.com, the author wrote about how Jim was a broke and struggling thespian once upon a time, so he took a blank check and made it out to himself. He wrote it in the amount of $10 million. He dated it 10 years from that moment. Each day he looked at his "trigger card" and knew that he would achieve his goal. In a decade, he was earning more than $10 million.

In the same way, you can use numerous things as your "trigger card." Making a trigger card is one of the best ways that has made a profound difference in my life. I'm able to interpret negative, toxic thoughts and to get back on track towards achieving my biggest goals at the moment. As Anthony Robbins once said, "Begin to live as though your prayers are already answered."

A General Point about Visualization

When you use any of these exercises, it's important to adhere to the same practices that make general visualization exercises so useful. In particular, it's vital to hold onto the feelings associated with your mental images and to allow these feelings to influence your everyday behaviors, thoughts, and actions.

Ever consider making a "dream board," or "vision board," as they are often called? They work, and there's actually a really simple explanation for why they work so well.

A dream board is a poster board with a collage of images that you can cut out of publications, draw, or create three-dimensional images using art supplies to glue onto the poster. The images represent your dreams and aspirations. You then hang or place your dream board in an area in your home or office where you can constantly see it on a daily basis. The idea behind it is that you become focused on your dreams.

Creating a sacred space that displays what you want actually does bring it to life. What we focus on expands. When you create a vision board and place it in a space where you see it often, you essentially end up doing short visualization exercises throughout the day. It can be used as a very powerful visualization tool, and with some thought, they don't take much effort to create. If you feel like you need more guidance with how to create your vision board, check out the Appendix at the end of the book for more information!

Being true to yourself and being able to enjoy life go hand-in-hand. The things that leave us hungry to discover the reason why—they are life-changing events. They teach us something we haven't known. Or they give us a gift we've never gotten before. Or they create an opportunity we've never even conceived of. This is how negative change gets transformed into positive change.

If you want to have more genuine pleasure, the first step is to let go of the past. The second step is to identify genuine sources of play and pleasure in your life. The third step, which is discussed in more detail in the next chapter, is to silence the voices in your head that make pleasure painful.

It is impossible to change yourself from the outside in. Real change happens from the inside out. One day you will wake up and realize that you have changed. Your insides will be different because of the steps you have made.

"You are only one step away from a totally different life."

—Author unknown

Journal Page

To wrap-up, write below one specific action step you will take to bring more passion into your life (make sure to include the due date this step must be completed by):

_____

_____

_____

_____

_____

_____

_____

_____

_____

_____

_____

_____

_____

_____

_____

_____

_____

_____

_____

Step 3: Ground Yourself

"To change your life, you have to change yourself. To change yourself, you have to change your mindset."

—Author unknown

When people identify what they truly want in their life, it can create some negative thoughts and feelings. In this chapter I will help you to identify what I like to call **visibility blocks**, and begin grounding these blocks. You will learn how to implement strategies that will guide you into a mindset for success. You will build confidence, strength, and courage to go after what you want—knowing you deserve it!

When we accept that there is something bigger meant for us and we begin talking about it with others, we may find that people we love and care about may respond negatively. Everybody will not celebrate you. When you have a dream, you're going to have some detractors.

People will get jealous, and may even attempt to make you look bad. They might try to talk you out of *your* dream because they are too afraid to chase their own. They may question your experience, talent, or capability to get that promotion. They may question your ability to be loved just because you've been married three times already.

Ugh! If I could tell you how many people were not in my corner during the times in my life where I made the biggest changes, it would blow your hair back. Let the words of unsupportive people go in one ear and out the other. It is so important to remember that other people don't determine your destiny. What stirs them up is the fact that you're moving forward, pursuing your destiny. They would love to convince you to keep your dream buried so you don't rise higher and make them look bad for not being bold enough to go after theirs. Instead of fulfilling their purpose, they focus on deterring you from living into yours.

Successful people, people that have a dream, don't waste their valuable time looking at what everybody else is doing; they're too busy focused on creating the life they have always desired.

The critics, the naysayers, and the detractors cannot stop your dreams. I say this respectfully, but sometimes the people closest to you will be the least supportive. Don't get distracted fighting battles that don't matter. Trying to prove to them who you are and trying to convince them how they should be towards you is just a waste of time. You don't need their approval. Let it go and chase your dream.

Bottom line, enemies target people who have a dream. They use oppositions, discouragement, delays, jealousy, everything they can to try to convince you to bury that dream.

If you're going to reach your highest potential, you have to make up your mind that you're in it for the long haul. You're not going to let people talk you out of your vision. Discouraging delays cause you to get distracted.

You're going to stay focused on your goal. Here's the key: you wouldn't have that opposition if you didn't have something great in you. If your dream wasn't alive and on track, you wouldn't have so many things coming against you. When "enemies" look at you, they say, "Oh no. Here comes another dreamer. Here comes another person full of faith, believing that they have seeds of greatness and are not stuck by their circumstances."

When you're a dreamer, you're dangerous to the enemy. You give them a nervous breakdown. They know you're headed to a new level; they know you're coming into an overflow. They know you're going to set a new standard for yourself. Here's the most important thing they know: there's nothing they can do to stop you! The forces that are for you are greater than the forces that are against you. However, the forces of opposition, along with your self-sabotaging thoughts, will work overtime trying to convince you to settle, to give in, and to remain where you are.

You have to remember this principle: when negative things happen, that's not stopping your destiny; that's a sign that you're on your way *to* your destiny. Every delay, every setback, and every disappointment did not, and will not, stop your dream. It's all a part of the process.

When you have a dream in your heart and when you are able to identify your purpose and passion, it doesn't mean that it's going to come to pass with no opposition, no delays, and no adversity. There will be things that you don't understand. You will have plenty of opportunities to get negative, but these are the times that it is most important to remember your purpose and your dreams.

Well, you might say, "Megan, I'm upset. I don't understand it. I got thrown into a pit."

"A friend lied about me."

"I lost a loved one."

"I went through a divorce."

Whatever your situation, it's just a detour on the way to your destiny. Don't worry, another caravan is coming to move you onto your next location.

When you face opposition, things don't go your way. Recognize that it's not permanent. That's not your final destination. Quit worrying about things that are only temporary. The injustice is temporary. The betrayal is not your permanent home. My challenge to you is to quit losing sleep over temporary stuff. Quit being discouraged over something that's only for a season. It's not permanent.

Over the past 20 + years of working in the mental health field and doing my own personal mindset work, I have done a ton of reading on belief systems, self-esteem, and self-image. I can't hide the fact that this is one of my favorite topics to speak about and to teach my clients. Honestly, it is one of the main reasons I wrote this book. Human beings struggle each day with what we say to ourselves.

If we take a minute to think about our own negative self-talk—both consciously and subconsciously—in a day, it is astounding! Why is it so easy for us to say something nice to someone else, but we can't do the same for ourselves? Why is loving ourselves so hard at times? The key is to be able to identify those negative thoughts, acknowledge them, and then to immediately replace the thoughts with something positive. This is what I call **thought stopping**.

I cannot imagine where I would be today if I let my struggles, negative thoughts, limiting beliefs, and negative reactions from people stop me from moving forward. I would probably still be in the fetal position on the floor crying. I have had to continuously "retrain" my brain over and over again through the years to remove these "cancerous" thoughts, especially when I found myself against a battle.

This is why I'm so excited for you to read this chapter! It is essential to show yourself compassion and to let go of negative thoughts. I am living proof that it is possible to turn off that negative mindset and to begin to believe *you are enough*!

In order to make effective long-term changes in your life, it is important to evaluate how easily your thinking can lead to self-sabotage. To make lasting changes, you need to embrace the power of thinking positively so the negative patterns do not come into play as you commit to moving forward.

The bottom line is that we seldom, if ever, achieve more than we believe ourselves to be capable of; more than what we believe we are worthy and deserving of; more than our belief in our ability to cope with life's challenges. There is a concept known as **belief-dependent realism**. Our beliefs shape our reality. Once we form our beliefs, our brains search for and find evidence to confirm them. We make ourselves right, which is why we often say, "Change doesn't feel right."

When reality pushes beyond the boundaries of our belief systems, we have a way of pulling it back in. When we believe in our unworthiness, life ponies up our precise valuations. When we don't believe we can handle life's challenges, we give up at the first obstacle. Limiting beliefs fabricate the fictions we routinely mistake for facts. They control the way we think, the way we talk to ourselves, and what we believe is possible.

Martin, a 24 year old—new entrepreneur and client of mine—wrote this about his mindset when he first began working with me:

Old stories and patterns have been big ones for me. I'm barely learning the power of my mind. I got so accustomed (and comfortable) replaying my own stories, that I didn't even realize until recently that I am totally capable of looking at life in new ways. I've had a profound realization that the "real world" is a mirror of my internal world. If I'm feeling down and allowing myself to be down, everything will seem to go wrong and I'll experience "bad luck." Conversely, if I'm thinking positive thoughts and boosting my self-esteem, amazing people (like you) and opportunities will meet me. I've felt completely stuck in my growth a few times in the last several years, and each time it's a mental game. The struggle for me has been letting go of my outdated beliefs about myself or the world around me. Right now, I feel as though I'm missing self-esteem and inner peace. I can fake (and do) charisma, sociability, and confidence. However, deep, deep down, I have work to do on my self-esteem. If I strengthen my core, I believe I will be unstoppable.

Martin has been able to learn and implement tools that have allowed him to retrain his brain to stop negative thinking. He has found a new level of self-esteem and self-confidence; it shows in the way he carries himself and the success he is achieving in his business. It makes me so very proud when I see this change happen in people.

Let's take a look at another person's life. Shelia. She is a work from home bookkeeper. She has plenty of high-paying clients and she loves what she does, but she wants to expand her business and become known as an industry expert. She'd like to start a podcast, and she already created the first few episodes outlined in detail.

However, Shelia went online to research how to start a podcast, and she gave up on the idea after an hour because her inner voice reminded her that she's not good with technology. Sheila didn't realize it, but she accepted a self-limiting belief.

Self-limiting beliefs are the ones that hold you back from achieving the very best in your business and in life. These beliefs are often so ingrained that it takes time to learn how to recognize them. Here are some warning signs that are self-sabotaging limiting beliefs in disguise:

1. **Self-Limiting Beliefs are Negative.** Self-limiting beliefs *are* always negative. It's the voice in your head that lists all of the reasons you won't succeed. You may think negative comments like, "Who are you to do this? Nobody is interested in what you say. You're too dumb to succeed. Everyone will laugh behind your back if you try to do this."

    You may not realize this, but these negative thoughts are often a defense mechanism. You never have to try if you believe that you're automatically going to fail; and if you don't try, then you don't have to risk getting hurt or failing.

2. **Self-Limiting Beliefs Encourage a Poverty Mindset.** Often, self-limiting beliefs leave you stuck with a poverty mindset. This goes beyond finances and affects how you live your life and run your business. Your inner voice might say things like, "There's only so much success to go around. I can't get ahead in business because my platform is tiny. All of my competitors are driving down the cost of my services, so I can't make a living wage."

   This type of poverty mindset keeps you fiercely guarding what's "yours." Not only does this keep you from growing your business, it keeps you from becoming friends with other solopreneurs. You see everyone as a "competitor" rather than a potential business partner or affiliate.

3. **Self-Limiting Beliefs Paint You as a Victim.** Self-limiting beliefs make you think you're a victim. For example, you might think things like, "Success isn't in my genes. I'm destined to be a loser. It doesn't matter how hard I work—I still won't be able to succeed."

   The problem with these thoughts is that they can convince you that you really are powerless. As a result, you don't challenge your self-limiting beliefs. You stay stuck in the same place for months, or even years, never realizing that the real problem was your mindset.

4. **Recognizing Self-Limiting Beliefs Takes Time.** When you find yourself focused on a self-limiting belief, try to counter it with a positive truth. Keep doing this, and eventually you'll notice a shift in your mindset that will lead to a stronger business and a better life. Where do self-limiting beliefs come from? Your mind is like a soundtrack. It constantly plays thoughts as you go through your day. You might have thought, "I'm too stupid to do this. My podcast is going to flop. I can't write compelling copy like other online business owners. I'm not successful enough to attend a seminar."

   If you've ever had thoughts like the ones above, then you've dealt with self-limiting beliefs. Self-limiting beliefs are the thoughts that hold you back from going after your business goals and prevent you from creating a life you love.

Don't think you have to give into these thoughts. Your thoughts are under your control. When you take the time to understand how self-limiting beliefs develop, you can gain insight and learn how to change your mental soundtrack.

5. **Unkind Remarks Can Result in Self-Limiting Beliefs.** Self-limiting beliefs can stem from unkind remarks from others. It may have been the teacher that told you that you were a terrible writer, the verbally abusive parent who called you a worthless child, or a friend who envies your life. Many people make the mistake of believing what they're told about themselves. They don't examine the belief when the words are said. This can cause you to carry around statements about your abilities that simply aren't true.

6. **Self-Doubt Can Lead to Self-Limiting Beliefs.** Everyone is insecure and doubts their own abilities at some point in their life. Maybe you weren't picked to work on a web design project you really wanted to do, so you assumed that your designs were terrible. Maybe you applied to be a speaker at an upcoming conference, and weren't chosen. During times of self-doubt, it's important to remember that other people's decisions are not a reflection of you. There are many reasons you may have missed out on the opportunity to work on a project or to speak at a seminar that had nothing to do with you. Maybe you weren't meant to work on that project because a better project is waiting for you. Maybe you weren't chosen to speak because you would've been in an auto accident if you would've traveled to the speaking engagement. Who knows?

7. **Your Perception of Others Can Cause Self-Limiting Beliefs.** Imagine this: you're at a networking event. You spot another small business owner in the crowd, and you walk

toward her. Before you can reach her, the business owner turns away. You assume she didn't want to talk to you. You might think things like, "I'm a poor conversationalist. No one's interested in me. Maybe she can tell I don't belong."

Your perception of this person keeps you from reaching out. So, you stick to talking with people you already know, and you miss out on the chance to build some great professional relationships. Learning how to change your mental soundtrack is essential if you want to reach the next level in your business. When you hear self-limiting beliefs, take a moment to consider if they're really true, or if they're simply lies that you've accepted as truth.

Identifying Cognitive Distortions or "Negative Thinking"

Cognitive distortions are simply ways that our mind convinces us of something that isn't really true. These inaccurate thoughts are usually used to reinforce negative thinking or emotions—telling ourselves things that sound rational and accurate, but really only serve to keep us feeling bad about ourselves. For instance, a person might tell themselves, "I always fail when I try to do something new; I therefore fail at everything I try."

This is an example of "black or white," or **polarized**, thinking. The person is only seeing things in absolutes—if they fail at one thing, they must fail at *all* things. If they added, "I must be a complete loser and failure" to their thinking, that would also be an example of **overgeneralization**—taking a failure at one specific task and generalizing it as their very self and identity.

Cognitive distortions are at the core of what many cognitive-behavioral and other kinds of therapists try to help a person learn to change in psychotherapy. By learning to correctly identify this kind of "stinkin' thinkin'," a person can then answer the negative thinking back, and refute it.

By refuting the negative thinking over and over again, it will slowly diminish overtime and be automatically replaced by more rational, balanced thinking. Not sure if your self-talk is positive or negative? Some common forms of negative self-talk include:

1. **Filtering.** You magnify the negative aspects of a situation and filter out all of the positive ones. For example, let's say you had a great day at work. You completed your tasks ahead of time and were complimented for doing a speedy and thorough job. That evening, you focus only on your plan to do even more tasks and forget about the compliments you received.

2. **Personalizing.** When something bad occurs, you automatically blame yourself. For example, you hear that an evening out with friends is canceled, and you assume that the change in plans is because no one wanted to be around you.

3. **Catastrophizing.** You automatically anticipate the worst. The drive-through coffee shop gets your order wrong, and you automatically think that the rest of your day will be a disaster.

4. **Polarizing.** You see things only as either good or bad. There is no middle ground. You feel that you have to be perfect or you're a total failure.

The following are examples of sabotaging thoughts that fast-paced individuals commonly make:

"I don't have enough time."

"I travel all the time for work."

"I have to entertain clients and eat out all the time."

"Watching what I eat is impossible."

Do any of these statements sound familiar? While all of them might be true, they are thoughts that stand in the way of us taking action. As a result of this type of thinking, losing weight can be very challenging. Instead of thinking you can't do something, try thinking the total opposite and telling yourself, "I can!"

It is important to try to stop yourself when you find yourself engaging in negative thinking. Be more flexible and compassionate towards yourself. It would feel much better to say, "I am really busy, but I can take some of my calls by cell phone and walk around."

"I do eat out a lot with my clients for business, but that does not mean I have to eat large portions or make unhealthy choices."

Thinking with less rigidity and judgment will allow you to move forward and make positive changes.

Journal Page

Finding out what limiting beliefs in your subconscious mind are holding you back from achieving the life you truly desire is essential. Take a few minutes to answer these questions in the space provided, or in your personal journal. The key here is to be 100% honest with yourself. Once you have accepted that these beliefs are currently holding you back, then you can change them by reprogramming new beliefs into your subconscious mind by using daily affirmations and other tools.

1. What limiting beliefs are holding you back?

_____

_____

_____

_____

2. What negative habits are holding you back?

_____

_____

_____

_____

3. Why do you believe that you are not good enough?

_____

_____

_____

_____

_____

_____

Understanding Positive Thinking and Self-Talk

Positive thinking doesn't mean that you keep your head in the sand and ignore life's less pleasant situations. Positive thinking just means that you approach unpleasantness in a more positive and productive way. You think the best is going to happen, not the worst.

Positive thinking often starts with self-talk. Self-talk is the endless stream of unspoken thoughts that run through your head. These automatic thoughts can be positive or negative. Some of your self-talk comes from logic and reason. Other self-talk may arise from misconceptions that you create because of lack of information.

If the thoughts that run through your head are mostly negative, your outlook on life is more likely pessimistic. If your thoughts are mostly positive, you're likely an optimist—someone who practices positive thinking.

The Health Benefits of Positive Thinking

Researchers continue to explore the effects of positive thinking and optimism on health. Health benefits that positive thinking may provide include:

- Increased life span.

- Lower rates of depression.

- Lower levels of distress.

- Greater resistance to the common cold.

- Better psychological and physical well-being.

- Better cardiovascular health and reduced risk of death from Cardiovascular disease.

- Better coping skills during hardships and times of stress.

It's unclear why people who engage in positive thinking experience these health benefits. One theory is that having a positive outlook enables you to cope better with stressful situations, which reduces the harmful health effects of stress on your body. It's also thought that positive and optimistic people tend to live healthier lifestyles—they get more physical activity, follow a healthier diet, and don't smoke or drink alcohol in excess.

Focusing on Positive Thinking

You can learn to turn negative thinking into positive thinking. The process is simple, but it does take time and practice—you're creating a new habit, after all. Here are some ways to think and behave in a more positive and optimistic way:

1. **Identify areas to change.** If you want to become more optimistic and engage in more positive thinking, first identify areas in your life that you usually think negatively about, whether it's work, your daily commute, or a relationship. You can start small by focusing on one area to approach in a more positive way.

2. **Check yourself.** Periodically during the day, stop and evaluate what you're thinking. If you find that your thoughts are mainly negative, try to find a way to put a positive spin on them.

3. **Be open to humor.** Give yourself permission to smile or laugh, especially during difficult times. Seek humor in everyday happenings. When you can laugh at life, you feel less stressed about it.

4. **Follow a healthy lifestyle.** Aim to exercise for about 30 minutes on most days of the week. You can also break it up into 10-minute chunks of time during the day. Exercise can positively affect mood and reduce stress. Follow a healthy diet to fuel your mind and body. And learn techniques to manage stress.

5. **Surround yourself with positive people.** Make sure those in your life are positive and supportive people you can

depend on to give helpful advice and feedback. Negative people may increase your stress level and make you doubt your ability to manage stress in healthy ways.

6. **Practice positive self-talk.** Start by following one simple rule: don't say anything to yourself that you wouldn't say to anyone else. Be gentle and encouraging with yourself. If a negative thought enters your mind, evaluate it rationally, and respond with affirmations of what is good about you. Think about things you're thankful for in your life.

Grounding Your Negative Thoughts

So, I know the real question you are asking is how do you change your thinking? You may find some of this information confusing or difficult to implement on your own, and that's okay.

I strongly encourage you to reach out to a coach or therapist who can help you through the process called **grounding**. Grounding is a technique where you rely upon special skills and techniques to gain control over your emotions so that you don't do something that you will regret. Secondly, grounding yourself gives you a new perspective of the current situation.

If you find yourself with a mind filled with racing, negative thoughts, using grounding techniques will deescalate your frenzied mental activity to help you divert yourself in healthy ways.

Not only will your mind be reset from the problems you're dealing with, you will also be better engaged to seek out productive solutions in the first place; you will begin to move from struggle into your strength!

6 Ways to Ground Yourself and Become Emotionally Stable:

1. **Increase your overall awareness.** Recognize when you are having these thoughts. In essence, you want to practice mindfulness and pay attention to what you are thinking and saying to yourself. It is crucial that you learn to recognize your inner critic without acting on it. If you are being mindful, then you are being aware.

2. **Challenge negative thoughts.**

3. **Replace the negative thoughts** with reasonable alternatives that are practical and realistic. The following is an example of how you can alter your thinking, and as a result, alter your fate:

   - **Thought:** "I ate something I shouldn't have. I might as well just start trying again tomorrow."

   - **Challenge:** "Does my whole day have to be ruined because I ate something I shouldn't have?'

   - **Helpful Response:** "I might have eaten something that wasn't good for me, but I can get right back on track and make a better choice for my next meal."

4. **Try something different this year:** *think differently.*

5. **Make a commitment towards taking small steps toward bigger goals.**

6. **Focus on what you can do each day to make yourself a priority.** I guarantee that you will be more productive and effective in all other areas of your life.

It's only when we shift our mindset about our health and life that we start seeing solid results. As discussed in previous chapters, it is vitally important to identify some of your mindset blocks.

Below are five of the most common blocks that might be holding you back, and how to overcome each of them.

Mindset Block #1: The "All or Nothing" Mindset

Have you ever skipped workouts just because you couldn't dedicate a whole hour to a gym class? Or decided you would start eating healthy tomorrow because you've already had two sodas *today*?

This is the **All or Nothing Mindset**, which is wrecking your attempts at becoming healthier in mind, body, and soul. You might be familiar with the term **perfectionism**—evident in wanting to make sure your blog posts, product, or design is perfect before it's out in the world.

The All or Nothing Mindset is closely related to perfectionism. I see almost everyone falling prey to this mindset because most people don't realize that all healthy habits have a positive impact, no matter how small they are.

I also struggle with this mindset, and often find myself having to revert back to my grounding skills. All these benefits will add up in the long run. Letting go of the All or Nothing Mindset can help you finally make progress toward your goals.

Overcome the All or Nothing Mindset by Starting Small & Staying Consistent

Set yourself up to win by starting small and staying consistent. You want to do this, especially if you have tried, but failed to maintain the healthy habit you're trying to build.

Start with an action so small that you just can't *not* complete it. It may be just five minutes of yoga or meditation every day, going for a walk, or maybe just adding veggies to a couple of meals each week. All of these are mindset grounding tools. Doing these small healthy habits consistently will train your brain to believe that you are someone who follows through on your intentions. This will help build the habit muscle, and you will be able to build better and healthier habits over time.

Mindset Block #2: The "I'm Busy" Mindset

We all know stress is bad for us, yet we wear it like a badge of honor. We are almost addicted to feeling stressed. We use "I'm busy" as an excuse for everything. Perhaps it makes us feel valuable, important, or useful. However, stress has a massive, negative impact on your health, energy levels, and productivity. Have you ever noticed how work seems effortless when you're feeling good, in control, and are enjoying what you're doing? But when you're stressed out, everything seems so hard.

Writing a blog post, or even a simple email, takes hours. You keep rewriting the same sentence over again without making any progress.

Stress is unavoidable and unpredictable; nevertheless, we can choose how we greet it. Don't let "I'm busy" become your crutch for not becoming healthier and more successful. What would change for you if every time you thought, "How is this happening for me," instead of, "Why is this happening to me?"

Could you see stress as an opportunity for growth? A fun test for your stress management skills?

Stop believing that you're "busy." Watch health and happiness come flooding into your life.

19 Tips to Overcome the I'm Busy Mindset

1. **Ask yourself, "What can I do about this?"**

2. **Smile often,** even if you feel silly, just start smiling. It decreases stress hormones and increases happiness.

3. **Practice gratitude daily.** It can transform your health, mood, and business.

4. **Create a weekly practice around stress management.** Try yoga, walking, meditation, tai chi, prayer, and any other contemplative techniques that resonates with you.

5. **Stop, drop, and belly breathe.** Deep belly breaths are your body's secret "off switch" for your fight-or-flight response. Set a timer to go off throughout the day, and when it does, take four deep belly breaths and switch your relaxation response back on.

6. **Exercise**—it's a proven stress buster!

7. **Eat real food** and avoid foods that actually increase cortisol (your stress hormone) production in your body—like sugar.

8. **Schedule, schedule, schedule.** Discipline creates freedom and can really help you feel in control of your life and business.

9. **"No" is a full sentence.** Try it out.

10. **Make time for things that bring you joy.** Make a list of these and schedule at least one per week.

11. **Get some sleep.** Being tired is stressful.

12. **Think about the five people you spend the most time with.** Do they make you feel motivated and alive, or drained and exhausted?

13. **Laugh more.**

14. **Play with animals.**

15. **Give generously.**

16. **Express yourself creatively.** It releases endorphins and other feel-good neurotransmitters.

17. **Have sex**—hey, it works.

18. **Alleviate loneliness** by calling a friend or family member. Join an online community or mastermind.

19. **Take radical action**—ask yourself what does my body need to heal? Listen to what it says. Maybe you need a new career, maybe you need to get that online biz off the ground, or you just need a change of scenery.

There is a quote from Brene Brown that I have hanging over my bed that I read every night before I go to sleep because I, too, struggle with the "I'm Busy" Mindset. It simply states: *"No matter how much I get done, or is left undone, at the end of the day I am enough."*

What does this mean to me? It reminds me that I am not perfect and do not have to be perfect. It reminds me that my to-do list will be there tomorrow; it doesn't make me a failure to not have everything checked off that list each night before I go to sleep. It reminds me to stop, take a deep breath, and engage in some grounding skills (meditation, affirmations, etc.) in order for me to turn off my mind and get a restful night's sleep.

Journal Page

Is there a quote or mantra that helps you slow down at the end of the day? Write it below:

_____

_____

_____

_____

_____

_____

_____

_____

_____

_____

_____

_____

_____

_____

_____

_____

_____

Mindset Block #3: The "I'm Not Good Enough" Mindset

Have you ever stopped and thought about the stories you might be telling yourself over and over again? Do you ever catch yourself saying, "I'm not good at sales" or "I'm not good with numbers?"

If you've been working on improving your mindset for your business or career, then you may already be aware of some of these negative beliefs and stories running in the background. But what about the negative beliefs you have with regards to your health? What sort of things do you say to yourself about your body? Are these stories helping you or holding you back?

The stories we tell ourselves create our subconscious identity. For example, thoughts like, "I am not the kind of person who can live on green smoothies" or "I am just not athletic enough to go running," are only holding you back from becoming healthier.

Although willpower can help (and is needed) to start new health habits, eventually your actions will reflect the beliefs you have about yourself. Your subconscious works to align your actions with your personal beliefs and identity. But you can use these stories to your advantage too. If you start believing that exercise makes you happier and more productive, you will make it a point to move more each day; you will make time for exercise. Healthy actions and habits become easier once they are aligned with the belief that you are someone who makes healthy choices. So get rid of the "I'm not good enough" self-talk.

If you remember from my personal story I shared in the beginning of the book, I struggled with this mindset for years—especially when it came to my ex-husband. I always thought I wasn't good enough, because if I was, he never would've had an affair. He never would've divorced me. This was the hardest to change; to change my thoughts of not being good enough to *I am enough*.

How did I do it? I practiced every… single… day multiple times a day to combat that thought by reminding myself of the good things about myself and the good things happening in my life. No matter what happens in my life—good, bad, or down right awful—I am the only one who can make myself feel "not good enough." I can now say with 100% certainty that *I am enough* for me, and that is all that matters.

Swap the Negative Self-Talk With a Positive Mindset to Become Healthier

Start becoming more aware. Write down the things that you are telling yourself about your health, career, relationships, and whatever you may be struggling with. Sometimes you have to take more than a few minutes to think about these negative messages. Anytime you find yourself having a negative thought, write it down.

Next, write out a positive affirmation about yourself and place it somewhere that you will be able to see it every day. When you hear yourself thinking or saying negative things, replace them by repeating a positive affirmation such as:

"I am someone who takes one step every day towards becoming a business owner."

"I am someone who is making healthy food choices each day to reach my weight loss goal."

Remember, your self-talk creates your reality. Be aware of what you are saying to yourself.

Mindset Block #4: The "Waiting to be Happy" Mindset

Society teaches us that happiness is conditioned-based. For example, once we get that promotion, once we lose the weight, once we get to a certain point in our lives, then we will be happy. This message is all around us. But what if it's actually the other way around?

What if getting into a positive mindset and doing what we love leads to becoming healthier, more productive, and successful?

A Harvard research study carried out by American Happiness Researcher, Author, and Speaker Shawn Achor showed that when our brain is positive we:

- Are three times more creative.

- Experience 31% higher levels of productivity.

- Are 40% more likely to receive a promotion at work.

- Achieve a 37 % higher level of sales.

- Experience more energy and see more opportunities when we have a positive mindset.

So, instead of waiting to be happy (once you've achieved a certain result), tune your mindset to be more positive.

Create a Daily Happiness Habit, Don't Wait for It

Happiness habits have been linked to greater success and energy—so much so that Shawn Achor wrote a book on the topic called *The Happiness Advantage*.

Stop believing that you will be happy once you are successful or once you are healthy; start being happy now, and it will help you achieve your goals. The best part is, these habits only take a few minutes to do. Pick one that resonates with you, and try it out for seven days:

- **Keep a daily gratitude journal.** Write down things you are grateful for in a notebook. Just make sure that each day you're writing about specific things you're grateful for.

- **Get daily exercise.** This one helps your health in many ways! Just do it!

- **Meditation.** Start with just five minutes each day. An app like Headspace is a good way to start if you are a beginner. You can also visit my blog for some great meditation strategies (www.missionstrenghsd.com/blog).

- **Perform random acts of kindness**, such as buying a stranger a cup of coffee or giving out compliments. It will not only make you feel good; I'm sure you will make the stranger's day too!

Mindset Block #5: The "Superhero" Mindset

If you're not happy with where your health and energy levels are at the moment, then the fastest way to get to where you want to be is to be held accountable. **Accountability**, in this regard, means taking actions towards specific goal(s) and involving others that reflect the integrity of the person you want to be.

In fact, Stanford University found that simply receiving a check-in phone call that asked about study participants' progress every two weeks, increased the amount of exercise participants did by 78% on average. The participants in the study who received those bi-weekly check-in phone calls were still exercising at the increased level even after 18 months.

Talk about sustainable results!

When I began writing this book I had to reach out for accountability partners to help me stay on track. It is so easy to get distracted with the craziness of life, but without my accountability partners, this book would've taken years to complete.

I've also had to ask for accountability partners when it came to struggles I was dealing with in life—especially when it came to working through the trauma I endured from Mr. N. I had to ask people to check-in on me, make sure I wasn't isolating myself, and that I was getting out of bed each morning. I would definitely not be where I am today if it wasn't for reaching out and asking for help.

Accountability can supercharge your results if you're having a hard time doing it yourself. Surrounding yourself with like-minded people, either through a group program, class, mentor, coach, or therapist, can help you reach your goals faster. So, get rid of your "cape," stop being a superhero, and leverage the power of accountability.

Overcome the "Superhero" Mindset by Staying Accountable

Do you have a friend who could go to the gym with you? Can you talk to your partner about the goals you have set for your future, and ask for support from him/her to keep you on track?

If not, then look into whether a coach, therapist, or a group program might be a good fit for you.

Journal Page

I want you to know that you don't have to do it all by yourself. Ask for accountability! Think about what you would desire in an accountability partner and what would help you to stay accountable. Write it below.

_____

_____

_____

_____

_____

_____

_____

_____

_____

_____

_____

_____

_____

_____

_____

_____

_____

_____

_____

_____

_____

_____

As we close out this chapter on grounding, I want to provide you with a summary of some of the grounding skills discussed in this chapter, as well as additional ideas not discussed. I want to challenge you to begin using some of these skills to begin defeating those negative thoughts and limiting beliefs about yourself. I guarantee that your life will begin to change!!!

1. **Coping cards:** Preparing coping statements and writing them onto coping cards that you carry with you makes sense. Whenever negative self-talk gets you down, pull out your coping card and read your positive affirmations until you feel better. It sounds too simple to work, *but it does work*, and since it's so simple, you can make your own cards right now.

2. **Create positive affirmations:** Affirmations are a statement of truth. What we say to ourselves is what we become. So let us be deliberate with our thoughts, words, and actions. Let us dream with our eyes open and be the example in the answer rather than passively waiting for something to come change us. We might be waiting for the rest of our lives. Let us be strong and win together. You can download the Top 100 Positive Affirmations that I created from my website: www.missionstrengthsd.com/affirmations

3. **Change your surroundings:** Make sure your surroundings are positive and supporting you towards your goals. The results in your life are a reflection of the 10 people you spend the most time with. Never forget that. Find accountability partners and mentors that support your goals and dreams!

4. **Practicing positive thinking every day:** If you tend to have a negative outlook, don't expect to become an optimist overnight. However, with practice, eventually your self-talk will contain less self-criticism and more self-acceptance. You may also become less critical of the world around you. When your state of mind is generally optimistic,

you're better able to handle everyday stress in a more constructive way. That ability may contribute to the widely observed health benefits of positive thinking.

We all have things that we're living for, something that we want to accomplish. Deep down, we know it's a part of our destiny. We can feel it so strongly. Along the way, we experience some setbacks. Maybe you didn't get the promotion you wanted, maybe the medical report wasn't good, or a relationship didn't work out. Life has a way of pushing down our dreams.

Our dreams can be buried under discouragement or past mistakes. There are dreams buried under divorce and low self-esteem. It's easy to settle for mediocrity, even though we have all this potential buried on the inside. Your dream may be buried, but the good news is that it's still alive. It's not too late to see it come to pass. We've all been through disappointments and setbacks. Life happens. But instead of remembering the hurt, the pain, or what didn't work out, the key to reaching your destiny is to remember your dream. It may seem impossible. Every voice even tells you that it's not going to happen.

However, if you'll do your part and start believing in *you* again, dreams that you've given up on are going to suddenly be exhumed. Problems that looked permanent are going to suddenly turn around.

Now don't let circumstances talk you out of it. You may not understand why a business didn't make it, why a person walked away, or why you came down with an illness. You were doing the right thing, but the wrong thing happened. It's all a part of the process—every disappointment, every delay, and every closed door. It's not just a setback; it's a setup for God to get you to where you're supposed to be. If your dream has been buried under the disappointments of the past, it's time to dust it off and dare to dream again! You're in a battle and it's time to stand up and fight. It's time to say, "I'm not going to let negative words come out of my mouth. I'm not going to let my own way of thinking stop me."

We can't be *conformed* to this world's culture. We can't be *conformed* to the wrong types of thinking. We have to be *transformed* by the renewing of our mind. The problem is our mind needs to catch up with what's going on in our spirits. We can do this by *not conforming* to our old thinking, but submitting ourselves to the idea that we are *enough*!

By learning new skills you are creating a mindset for success. You will see more potential and take more action. This will give you more results, and as a result, you will build confidence, strength, and courage to go after what you want and know you deserve it.

"Living a brave life is not always easy. We stumble and we fall. It is the rise from the falling that makes us strong!

—Brene Brown

Journal Page

What are some grounding skills that you would like to begin implementing in your life to help you break through those blocks that are keeping you stuck? When will you start these skills? How often will you practice these skills each day? Spend time writing about how grounding skills can help move you from being stuck to *you are enough*!

_____

_____

_____

_____

_____

_____

_____

_____

_____

_____

_____

_____

_____

_____

_____

_____

_____

_____

_____

_____

Step 4: Developing Your Strength Plan

"You owe yourself the love that you so freely give to others."

—Author unknown

This chapter focuses on what I like to call **Your Strength Plan**. In this chapter I help you identify what skills you need to include in your daily life to help strengthen your mind, body, and soul.

We live in a society that loves achievement, qualifications, status, and success. Many people work extremely hard to get there—ignoring what their bodies and minds are telling them. But what's the point of success and a great career if you're always stressed, overwhelmed, don't see much of your family and friends, or you're simply grumpy/tired when you actually do see them?

Sadly, life balance and self-care are often seen as "soft" requirements—something high achievers don't (or shouldn't) need. We get the message we should just be able to soldier on through illness and stress. We are told that if we take a holiday, go on a city break, have a bubble bath, or sleep in on Sundays, that we aren't being very productive. After all, a successful person should have this under control. Too much self-care is a sign of weakness, or perhaps seen as selfish or indulgent.

For anyone seeking to live a healthy and sustainable life, one vital habit is **self-care**. When we are living lives filled with activity, noise, and hurry, it is incredibly difficult to feel healthy and rested. When that is our overall experience with life, the result is that we become stressed and burned out. In order to nurture the health of our mind, body, and soul, we need to re-center and restore. We need these in short spurts throughout the day, as well as in longer stretches of time as needed. The thing about self-care is that it is a practice that requires you choosing to do it. It will not happen unless you intentionally make space for it. But the result is worth the effort.

Life without self-care and life balance can be pretty miserable, as it can lead to a life that lacks joy and substance. Self-care is what your Strength Plan is all about! During this part of your journey, we will assess your balance and self-care needs, identify what's getting in the way, and finally implement self-care strategies that will help you enjoy your life more!

Self-care is *crucial* for your physical, emotional, and mental well-being. Below I provide a list of how self-care, or the lack thereof, can impact you.

Reasons You Should **Not** *Neglect Self-Care*

- **Know your worth.** Self-care helps maintain a healthy relationship with yourself, as it produces positive feelings and boosts your self-confidence.

- **Healthy work-life balance.** Work self-care habits can include intermittent breaks (5-minute recess), setting professional boundaries, and avoidance of overextending.

- **Stress management.** Constant stress and anxiety can have an adverse effect on your mental and physical health. Smart self-care habits, like eating healthy, connecting with a loved one, or practicing meditation cuts down the toxic effects of stress by improving your mood and boosting energy and confidence levels.

- **Start living, stop existing.** Life is a precious gift. So why waste it when we have the choice to have a more meaningful existence? We have a lot of responsibilities, but it is important to remember that taking care of yourself is also your responsibility.

- **Better physical health.** Self-care is not just about your mental health. It is also about caring for your physical self by eating healthy, getting adequate sleep, caring about your hygiene, and exercising regularly.

First, it is important to **assess** your balance and self-care needs. Secondly, you need to **identify** what's getting in the way of maintaining self–care. Finally, you need to **develop** and **implement** self-care strategies that will help you enjoy your life more!

Action is a key word to achieving your dreams. If you take action by using the right emotional vibration, your results will show up much quicker than if you take action using negative emotional vibration. For example, frustration, impatience, anger, or perfectionism. The key is to start your day positively and make feeling good a priority by truly loving yourself.

On the next few pages, I share some self-care tips I have found useful for myself, as well as for my clients.

Self-Care Tip #1: Morning Rituals

How many times have you "woken up on the wrong side of the bed?" These groggy, unproductive, and messy mornings are usually the result of poor planning, or a lack of a solid morning routine.

Morning routines not only instill a sense of purpose, peace, and ritual into your day, but they ensure that you're getting your goals accomplished, and they give you a solid foundation for whatever the day throws at you.

We all wake up with a blank slate—a chance to have an awesome and productive day! Having a steady ritual will set you on this path. Picture a bowl of blueberries. This is the mental energy you wake up with each day. Every decision you make throughout the day—no matter how small— costs you a blueberry. You can spend your bowl however you like.

With that in mind, what if every morning you're deciding whether to press snooze again, whether you should scroll your Facebook feed, or whether to go to the gym? What if you're always in decision mode the moment you wake up? What if you had to make a decision whether or not to go to the gym each morning? The dialogue in your head would sound something like, "Oh no, wait it's too cold, but it will make me feel more alive, but it's so far away, but health is important to me…"

Blueberry, blueberry, blueberry.

That's why morning rituals can be really helpful. Your rituals keep you committed. When you create a morning ritual, you reduce the amount of choices you have to make—saving your precious mental energy for bigger, brighter things.

I have created some examples to help you jump start your mornings, including how to immediately have more energy, how to have more clarity and awareness, and how to reduce stress and anxiety. Your morning ritual could include:

- **Breathing.** Sit comfortably with your back straight. Count 1-2-3-4 while taking a deep breath in, then counting 1-2-3-4 when breathing out. Breathe in through your nose and out through your mouth. Do this 10-15 times.

- **Fuel your body.** Drink three full glasses of water.

- **Gratitude.** Simply close your eyes. Put your hand on your heart, and visualize 3-5 things/people you are grateful for. Another option is to write a gratitude list in your journal.

- **Affirmations.** Repeat out loud at least five positive self-statements that you believe about yourself (download the Top 100 Positive Affirmations at: www.missionstrengthsd.com/affirmations).

- **Manifestation.** Make a dedication for the day. This could be an emotional state you want to bring forth within you (courage, love, patience, gratitude) or a higher intention for the 24 hours ahead of you (to show kindness, face fears, or focus on your goals). Refer to the Questions to Empower Your Day in the appendix section of this book for more ideas on how to manifest each day!

- **Love energy.** Write an acronym or symbol for your daily dedication on the back of your hand, or put it as your phone screensaver using an app like Word Swag or A Beautiful Mess. It will serve as your gentle reminder throughout the day to stay on track, and to not get lost down rabbit holes that don't match who you are or your vision for your dream life.

Self-Care Tip #2: Relationships

You will realize that there is a purpose for each person you meet. Some will test you and some will teach you. But most important are the ones who bring out the best in you. Those are the ones worth keeping around.

In the course of our lives, we spend most of our time with just five people! Success experts say that *who* we spend our time with is a key influence on our happiness—and whether we succeed or fail. Some relationships uplift and inspire us, and others are downright draining.

Some people can be mean and will try to take their issues out on you. Avoid those people. Their attitude towards you is more about their own struggles and fears than it is about you. Send them some compassion, but don't allow yourself to be their punching bag.

When I was dealing with all of the drama with Mr. N, I constantly felt drained physically and emotionally. I was so focused on trying to make our relationship work that I forgot about the relationship with myself. I was not eating right, I lost weight, I gained weight, I hardly slept, I was on edge all of the time, I got more grey hair, and the list goes on.

Once I was able to accept the fact that Mr. N's behaviors and actions towards me was more about him than it was about me, I was able to begin to recognize the damage this relationship was having on me—not just mentally, but physically as well.

Toxic relationships can literally make our bodies unhealthy. We need to be aware and be intentional with whom we spend our time. The people in our lives can either help us or hinder us. We have to learn to set boundaries with others to ensure that we are taking care of ourselves first.

Yes, there's a time for caring for others, but it's *equally*, if not more important, to take time for you too. Taking time for yourself is not about being selfish. It's about rejuvenating yourself so that you can be better for others around you.

Journal Page

Take the time to evaluate your relationships. Which ones feel like they're adding to your life and which ones feel like they're subtracting from it?

_____

_____

_____

_____

_____

_____

_____

_____

_____

_____

_____

_____

_____

_____

_____

_____

_____

_____

_____

_____

_____

Self-Care Tip #3: Time Management

Many people work extremely hard to make a success of their lives, but are they working *effectively*? Could they be more productive if they managed their time better? The answer is almost definitely "yes."

It's all about awareness. You can teach someone as many time management tricks and techniques as you like, but without awareness—without the knowledge of what they currently do and how they sabotage themselves—they're going to continue making the same mistakes. And without understanding their priorities, and working on these priorities first, people's lives are going to fill up with less important tasks and more obstacles. Ultimately, this is very dissatisfying. Furthermore, this lack of satisfaction is often why people come to coaching—to achieve goals, dreams, and be held accountable to make meaningful changes in their lives.

Life is not all about productivity and being effective. There are many other important things, like relationships, inner peace, life balance, fun, and being of service. This toolkit is not intended to promote the idea that you should work even harder and achieve more; it's about helping you to be more effective with the time you have.

Your priorities in life are a mixture of both work and personal. These tools will help you to learn and identify what really matters—across your life and work. And then you will have the tools and awareness to ensure that priorities are prioritized!

Strategies to Help You Get More Out of Each Day:

Make A Monthly Action Plan

1. Fill in your goals for the month and visualize yourself achieving your goal.
2. Re-write your *why* at the beginning of each month.
3. Set a reward for yourself if you achieve your goal.
4. Reflect. Answer the following questions at the end of each month to help you reflect:

» What did I learn from this month?
» Distractions/Mental Blocks.
» How did I make myself feel good?
» What did not happen? Why?
» What actions can I take to improve?
» People I learned from and who inspired me.
» What are the greatest insights that I have gained over the past month?
» What obstacles or fears did I encounter inside myself?
» What did I learn from watching my emotional vibrations daily? What was the most common negative emotion?
» Did I fully enjoy whatever I was doing this month? Was I really "here," or was I just showing up? How can I be more present?

Make A Weekly Action Plan

1. Fill in your **goals** for the week.
2. **Visualize** yourself achieving that goal.
3. Fill in your top **3 priorities** for each day.
4. Write down your personal to-do list for the week.
5. Include **action steps** you will take during the week.
6. **Reward** yourself each day for accomplishing your little goals!

Scheduling. Effective scheduling is one of the most important time management skills you can use! Scheduling is the process by which you plan the use of your time. In order to schedule efficiently, you need an effective scheduling system. There are a variety of options to choose from, including a diary, calendar, planner, PDA, or software such as MS Outlook. CTools also has a calendar function. Keep in mind that self-care should be scheduled into your time.

Scheduling is then a five-step process:

1. Identify the time you have available.
2. Block in the essential tasks you must carry out.
3. Schedule in high priority urgent tasks and vital "house-keeping" activities.

4. Block in appropriate time to handle unpredictable situations, events and/or circumstances.
5. In the time that remains, schedule the activities that address your priorities and personal goals.

Ending Procrastination. There is no time for procrastination while getting your MSW! Time flies by so quickly, so don't wait until Thanksgiving break to start your fall semester assignments. You must try to minimize or end your procrastinating ways early! So to overcome procrastination, you must first recognize that you're doing it, then figure out why, and lastly get over it! Here are some simple steps to help identify and overcome procrastination.

1. *Step 1:* Recognize that you're procrastinating. If you're honest with yourself, you'll be able to know when you're procrastinating. Below are some common warning signs:
   » Filling your day with low priority tasks from your to-do list.
   » Immediately going to get coffee or check emails when sitting down to start a high-priority task.
   » Leaving an item on your to-do list for a long time, even though you know it's important.
   » Saying "yes" to unimportant tasks that others ask you to do to fill your time with these instead of completing your important tasks.

2. *Step 2:* Figure out why you're procrastinating. The two common reasons for procrastination are:
   » **Finding the task unpleasant.** If you are putting off a task because you just don't want to do it, you need to find ways of motivating yourself. The following approaches can be helpful: Make your own rewards. For example, promise yourself a trip to the mall or a tasty snack if you complete a certain task. Ask someone else to check up on you. Peer pressure works! Identify the negative consequences of *not* doing the task.
   » **Finding the task overwhelming.** If you're putting a task off because it's overwhelming, here are some tips:

Break the project into smaller, more manageable tasks. Start with some quick, small tasks, even if these are not the logical first actions. This will make you feel as though you are achieving things, and perhaps the whole project won't be so overwhelming.

Self-Care Tip #4: Make it Simple

It's the constant repetition of many tiny habits, which together soothe you and make sure you're at your optimum—emotionally, physically, and mentally. The best way to do this is to implement tiny self-care habits every day. To regularly include in your life a little bit of love and attention for your own body, mind, and soul.

Author Ellen Bard created a list of tiny self-care activities for your mind, body and soul that you can fit into a short amount of time, usually with little cost. I challenge my clients to pick one from each category, and to include them in their week. I challenge you to do the same!

Tiny Self-Care Ideas for the Mind

1. *Start a compliments file.* Document the great things people say about you to read later.

2. *Scratch off a lurker on your to-do list*, something that's been there for ages and you'll never do.

3. *Change up the way you make decisions.* Decide something with your heart if you usually use your head. Or if you tend to go with your heart, decide with your head.

4. *Go cloud-watching.* Lie on your back, relax, and watch the sky.

5. *Take another route to work.* Mixing up your routine in small ways creates new neural pathways in the brain to keep it healthy.

6. *Pay attention to something you usually do on autopilot*, perhaps brushing your teeth, driving, eating, or performing your morning routine.

7. *Goof around for a bit.* Schedule in five minutes of "play" (non-directed activity) several times throughout your day.

8. *Create a deliberate habit*, and routinize something small in your life by doing it in the same way each day. For example, what you wear on Tuesdays, picking up the dental floss before you brush, or double-checking to make sure you locked your front door.

9. *Fix a small annoyance at home that's been nagging you*—a lost button, a drawer that's stuck, or a light bulb that's gone.

10. *Punctuate your day with a mini-meditation* with one minute of awareness of your thoughts, feelings, and sensations; one minute of focused attention on breathing; and one minute of awareness of the body as a whole.

11. *Be selfish.* Do one thing today just because it makes you happy.

12. *Do a mini-declutter.* Recycle three things from your wardrobe that you don't love or regularly wear.

13. *Unplug for an hour.* Switch everything to airplane mode, and free yourself from the constant *bings* of social media and email.

14. *Get out of your comfort zone*, even if it's just talking to a stranger at the bus stop.

15. *Edit your social media feeds, and take out any negative people.* You can just "mute" them; you don't have to delete them.

Tiny Self-Care Ideas for the Body

1. *Give your body ten minutes of mindful attention.* Use the body scan technique to check in with each part of your body.

2. *Oxygenate by taking three deep breaths.* Breathe into your abdomen and let the air puff out your stomach and chest.

3. *Get down and boogie.* Put on your favorite upbeat record and shake your booty.

4. *Stretch out the kinks.* If you're at work, you can always head to the bathroom to avoid strange looks.

5. *Run (or walk, depending on your current physical health) for a few minutes.* Or go up and down the stairs three times.

6. *Narrow your food choices.* Pick two healthy breakfasts, lunches, and dinners and rotate for the week.

7. *Activate your self-soothing system.* Stroke your own arm, or if that feels too weird, moisturize.

8. *Get to know yourself intimately.* Look lovingly and without judgment at yourself naked. Use a mirror to make sure you get to know all of you!

9. *Make one small change to your diet for the week.* Drink an extra glass of water each day, or have an extra portion of veggies each meal.

10. *Give your body a treat.* Pick something from your wardrobe that feels great next to your skin.

11. *Be still.* Sit somewhere green, and be quiet for a few minutes.

12. *Get fifteen minutes of sun,* especially if you're in a cold climate. Use sunscreen, if appropriate.

13. *Inhale an upbeat smell.* Try peppermint to suppress food cravings, and to boost mood and motivation.

14. *Have a good laugh.* Read a couple of comic strips that you enjoy. For inspiration, try Calvin and Hobbes, Dilbert, or Xkcd.

15. *Take a quick nap.* Ten to twenty minutes can reduce your sleep debt and leave you ready for action.

Tiny Self-Care Ideas for the Soul

1. *Imagine you're your best friend.* If you were, what would you tell yourself right now? Look in the mirror and say it.

2. *Use your commute for a "Beauty Scavenger Hunt."* Find five unexpected beautiful things on your way to work.

3. *Help someone.* Carry a bag, open a door, or pick up an extra carton of milk for a neighbor.

4. *Check in with your emotions.* Sit quietly, and just name— without judgment—what you're feeling.

5. *Write out your thoughts.* Go for fifteen minutes on anything bothering you. Then let it go as you burn or bend the paper.

6. *Choose who you spend your time with today.* Hang out with "Radiators" who emit enthusiasm and positivity, and not "Drains" whose pessimism and negativity robs energy.

7. *Stroke a pet.* If you don't have one, go to the park and find one. Of course, ask first! People can be sensitive about their pets.

8. *Get positive feedback.* Ask three good friends to tell you what they love about you.

9. *Make a small connection.* Have a few sentences of conversation with someone in customer service such as a sales assistant or barista.

10. *Splurge a little.* Buy a small luxury as a way of valuing yourself.

11. *Have a self-date.* Spend an hour alone doing something that nourishes you (reading, a hobby, visiting a museum, or gallery, etc.)

12. *Exercise as a signature strength.* Think about what you're good at, and find an opportunity for it today.

13. *Take a home spa.* Have a long bath or shower, sit around in your bathrobe, and read magazines.

14. *Ask for help*—big or small, but reach out.

15. *Plan a two-day holiday for next weekend.* Turn off your phone, tell people you'll be away, and then do something new in your own town.

The examples above are a few of the many ways you can show yourself some love. Some are just basic human needs and seem like common sense, but all of them have been shown to support one's mood. And you don't have to do them all.

With a little bit of attention to your own self-care, the fog will lift. You'll feel more connected to yourself and the world around you. You'll delight in small pleasures, and nothing will seem quite as difficult as it did before.

Like a car, you must keep yourself tuned up to make sure that you don't need a complete overhaul. Incorporating a few of these tiny self-care ideas in your day will help keep you in tune.

People often ask me what my self-care looks like. The word that encompasses my self-care is **prioritizing.** I make both adequate sleep and exercise high priorities, regardless of what's going on in my life or how busy I am.

On a daily basis, I write three things I'm grateful for, three affir-mations, I write a biography of myself from the future as if someone was reading it about me, then I write a journal entry from my future describing all the happenings of my day and the feelings evoked.

I remind myself that by compromising these things, I compromise my mental and physical wellness, as well as my effectiveness in every area of life. I also set aside some time and money for regular massage, which has a broad range of mental and physical health benefits—oh, and of course it feels awesome!

I schedule my wellness, my time off, and my self-care like I sched-ule work and appointments. I don't use my phone calendar; instead, I use a hand written planner. Why? Because it works! When I used to use my phone calendar, I would get overwhelmed and stressed out with all the things I had to do. I would always think there is just not enough time in the day to get everything done. Now I use a planner with 30-minute increments. This allows me to schedule my appoint-ments, to-do lists, and self-care daily. I'm able to see little bits of time here and there throughout each day that are not actually scheduled. I have found that it has lowered my stress immensely!

So, even though you're probably doing some self-care already (woohoo for you!), it's easy to skip or forget when times are tough. Remember to take care of yourself all of the time. No matter what's going on, you always deserve it.

Our thoughts become our reality. Get your thoughts to the place you want to be, and your physical reality will eventually catch up. I promise you. And always remember, you *are* doing enough. You *are* enough. And all the answers you need are already inside of you. You just need to create the space to listen. This will help.

Also, always remember that it isn't selfish to love yourself. Take care of yourself and make your happiness a priority. It is necessary.

"When you recover or discover something that nourishes your soul and brings joy, care enough about yourself to make room for it in your life."

—Jean Shinoda Bolen

Journal Page

Write a response to the following writing prompt. You may need extra writing space than what is provided on this page. Please feel free to grab a sheet of paper or to use your journal. At the bottom of this page, is guidance to help you get the most out of this prompt.

What I *really* need for my own sense of well-being, replenishment, stress release and/or inner peace at this time is...

_____

_____

_____

_____

_____

_____

_____

_____

Guidance

1. Pause and simply listen to what guidance you are receiving from within and from your spirit (universal energy source).

2. Start writing. Simply capture what you are hearing from within.

3. Keep your pen moving for at least 15 minutes—just keep listening within and writing.

4. Don't worry about grammar or making high art. You're writing for yourself, writing to hear your own thinking, your own knowing, and to connect with your authentic needs. Simply keep your pen moving and trust the process. Trust yourself.

Journal Page

Read over what you just wrote, and now write for five more minutes using this writing prompt to guide you.

What is clear to me now is...

_____

_____

_____

_____

_____

_____

_____

_____

_____

_____

_____

_____

_____

_____

_____

_____

_____

_____

_____

_____

Journal Page

Choose *one* action you would like to take based on the insights you gained from your reflective journaling exercise on the previous two pages. Give yourself permission to be spontaneous!

Step 5: Strengthening Your Healthy Habits

"Feel the Present, hold the vision, let go of resistance, enjoy the journey, trust the process and know that all is well."

— Frederik Talloen

It's normal for challenges and mindset blocks to creep in at any time—even when things are going good for us. When limiting beliefs come up, it's important to have a plan in order to strengthen all the habits you have created through your work in this program. The last and final step does just that.

You will develop a **maintenance plan**, which includes identifying when you need redirection or grounding so that you can hit the "reset" button on your mindset. Of course, your personalized plan will include stress management tips, as well as motivational and inspiring tools designed specifically for you!

A Strength Plan means adding good things into your life, including self-care, support groups, and regularly scheduled fun (and safe) things to do. A maintenance plan, also known as preventive, or cyclical maintenance, is an essential part of the ongoing care and upkeep of your overall health and wellbeing.

During the maintenance stage, your initial goals have been achieved, and in this stage the goal is to preserve your new lifestyle. You continue to track your progress and stay focused on your goals. You like the "new skin" you're in, and strive to stay here, reflecting on everything you've accomplished. This is your new normal.

The aim of this stage is to also help you get to a position where you can maintain the maintenance stage and sustain your new, healthier lifestyle. But for many people, this is the hardest part, even harder than making the initial changes. It's about trying to ensure you don't slip back into your old behaviors. Maybe you skip a day of self-care, which is okay if it's just one day, but one day can turn into one week, then one month, and so forth. It's vital for you to recognize that it's very easy to reintroduce the same old and unhealthy habits into your lifestyle—almost without even noticing it.

The maintenance stage also includes tweaks and improvements to your Strength Plan as well as taking on new challenges. For example, that 15-minute daily walk might turn into 30 minutes, and eventually, even some jogging. These incremental changes are good and healthy once the initial actions have proven to take hold and have become habit.

Another aspect of the maintenance stage is finding ways to stay motivated. A once-exciting fitness routine or eating plan can become stale. When this happens, there is risk of digressing back to old patterns—don't let this happen!

Sometimes we find ourselves dealing with **complacency**. Dictionary.com's definition of Complacency is a feeling of smug or uncritical satisfaction with oneself or one's achievements. To say an individual is acting "complacently" means that they are taking things for granted. They have developed a type of smugness over their achievements, and they just expect that things will remain the same forever. When an individual becomes complacent, they no longer feel that they need to work in order to find success in life—they view it as something they have already earned.

Complacency can creep into our lives when we are not paying attention to our mindset and the things we are telling ourselves. When someone begins to take for granted the work they have done in order to create the life they truly wanted, they can find themselves back to feeling stuck and unmotivated.

Paying close attention to distorted and self-limiting beliefs, lack of self-care, feelings of overwhelm and stress, and situations that tend to cause those thoughts and feelings, is key to continued success. Without a strong commitment to maintenance, there will surely be slips back into old thinking patterns.

During this stage, it's important to identify early warning signs and triggers (both positive and negative) that may affect your mindset. This should be somewhat of an easy task now that you have worked through some of your limiting beliefs. Ask yourself if you're engaged in your daily life or if you're just going through the motions. Are you back to settling for the status quo instead of thriving?

Bonnie Marcus, an executive coach talks about some warning sign of complacency.

1. **You aren't learning.** Every single day should be treated as a learning experience, an opportunity to acquire a new set of knowledge and skills and to build upon the foundation that already exists. Complacent people are content with what they already know or do, and consequently, don't seek out new information or experiences.

2. **You aren't challenging yourself.** A challenge can be something as big as learning a new language, or as small as making it through a book you've been meaning to read. It's about pushing yourself to do things that are as difficult as they are rewarding. Complacency holds people back from challenging themselves.

3. **You stop trying new things.** New experiences are what life is all about. Travelling, trying different jobs, meeting new people, eating foreign food, and so on. You'll never know what you're missing unless you take the plunge, and try something new! Complacency prevents people from feeling that urge to go out and seek an unprecedented experience.

4. **You lose ambition.** It's great to have dreams and ambitions, but if you aren't actively working towards achieving them, then that's all they will ever be. Unfulfilled dreams and ambitions. A lack of ambition is an absence of drive and passion to do and be better. To realize a dream and strive to attain it would be highly uncharacteristic of someone who suffers from complacency.

5. **You stop growing.** We all stop growing at some point, physically speaking. But you should never stop growing intellectually or spiritually. Think of complacency as a roadblock on your journey to become who you are.

Share this information with individuals in your support network so if/when your mindset shifts, they know what to look for and how to respond. They know how to encourage you to stay on track. In other words, make a promise and have someone check in on you to see if you're keeping that promise. It might be to sign up for a class or it might be to make a phone call. Whatever it is, have someone to answer to, and you will see how this has a positive impact on your end goal. Accountability is key when it comes to maintaining the life we have created for ourselves, and it's a great way to keep moving forward and maintaining good habits.

This is something that I found so incredibly helpful when I was working through the *5 Steps* after my divorce. I reached out to my friends, and shared with them my warning signs of complacency and other parts of my Strength Plan so they knew how to support me.

It's important to note that an individual who is complacent isn't the same as saying they're confident. This is because complacency is a false type of confidence, and it doesn't reflect reality. A truly confident person fully understands their deficits, as well as their assets. This means they are acting in a rational manner. Those individuals who are building a successful life have every right to feel confident. As long as they continue to do productive things, their success is almost guaranteed, and there isn't a need for them to do anything to make this happen.

The anecdote to complacency is gratitude. This is your ability to acknowledge all of the good people and things in your life, and to not take them for granted. Gratefulness means that you feel humble enough to appreciate what you have. It also means that you are willing to keep on working to maintain such favorable conditions. Gratitude is an incredible skill that will help you remain grounded and focused.

As you move forward in your journey, it's important that you're honest with yourself so that you can adapt and continue to create a lifestyle that is conducive to your health. Mind. Body. Soul.

When something small threatens to destroy your attitude and positive outlook, think about the fact that everyone makes mistakes. Whether it is yourself or someone else who caused the situation that feels like a train wreck, keep in mind that mistakes are a normal part of life that happen to everyone. Don't let one bad moment take you by surprise.

Remember, you're human and don't have to be perfect. So, when you encounter a bump in the road (and yes, there will be bumps), go back to your Strength Plan, and then revisit the skills you have used to get this far. Give yourself grace and remember *you are enough!*

> *"Don't die by your weaknesses, live*
> *through your strengths."*

> — Mark S. Kerr

Journal Page

What areas in your life do you think you could fall into complacency? What are the steps you will take to get back on track if you find yourself slipping back into old thinking patterns? Who will keep you accountable?

_____

_____

_____

_____

_____

_____

_____

_____

_____

_____

_____

_____

_____

_____

_____

_____

_____

_____

_____

Afterward: Emearging from the Mud

"Strength does not come from winning. Your struggles develop your strengths. When you go through hardships and decide not to surrender, That is strength!"

—Mohandas Gandhi

I began writing this book six months ago in the midst of me saying goodbye to the story I was allowing Mr. N to create for me. This has been the most intense and difficult project I've ever undertaken, but it has also been the most rewarding.

June 2015 changed my life forever. My heart and life were shattered into a million pieces. It was then that I began working these *5 Steps* that allowed me to begin to dream again. I was faced with other intense struggles, including losing a job that I loved, moving to San Diego, and encountering financial issues. But it was these *5 Steps* that allowed me to stay focused on my future, that allowed me to begin my journey into entrepreneurship, and they were the reason I began creating a life that I loved.

Then, of course, I was hit with yet again more drama and chaos with Mr. N, and again I was back to "Step 1." I had to recreate a new vision for my life, a new hope. It still included my mindset coaching business and my network marketing business, but with working through these steps again, I was able to find another purpose for my life. That purpose was writing this book.

As I sit here putting the final touches on these pages, I'm happy to say that I've begun a new chapter in my life. I've not had any type of contact with Mr. N since February of 2018. I believe that everything happens for a reason, and even though I was sad and heartbroken from how our relationship ended, I truly believe that this book could not have been created if Mr. N was still in my life.

I'm finally the person I was striving so hard to become for so many years, yet was never able to fully evolve into that person before because I was letting my fear and my limiting beliefs to keep me stuck. My fear was killing my dreams. My fear was killing my hope. My fear was holding me back from doing the things I knew within myself I was capable of doing. Fear had me paralyzed. I finally took control of my life and began working through these *5 Steps*. I have *finally* emerged from the mud and into a new sense of being. A new sense of victory and excitement. I can finally say that I am so thankful for the struggles I have endured because they have allowed me to truly become the person I was always meant to be.

I am enough. These simple words come from a deep, little secret space in my heart. It took a lot of time and many tears to finally come to this humble, understated, beautiful belief. From accepting and re-believing that I am truly enough came deep transformation, strength, and self-love. Being enough means that I am great the way I am. It means that I'm worthy of happiness, love, and respect.

As I was writing this "Afterward," I was on the phone with one of my closest friends— Jacquelyn. We were talking about the book, and she asked me, "Megan, who is in your strength?"

That question stopped me dead in my tracks. I loved it! It was such a profound question! I began to think about all of the people in my life who have been here for me day in and day out through all of my struggles. I'm so incredibly blessed to have some spectacular people in my life who have helped me move from my struggles *into* my strength!

I truly believe that people are placed in your life at the exact moment you need them the most. During the journey towards closure with Mr. N, I was re-united with my friend Theresa who I've known since high school. We reconnected on social media, and I discovered that she was going through the same drama with her now ex-boyfriend as I was going through with Mr. N. We have now re-created an amazing friendship. A friendship where we support one another in staying true to ourselves. This never would have happened if I had not let go of my past and Mr. N.

Since being able to visualize my desire for entrepreneurship and my coaching business, I've met such phenomenal and inspiring people through my network marketing business, attending women empowering events, and doing speaking engagements. People I know would not have crossed my path if I continued to allow myself to remain stuck in the mud—just going through life with no real sense of who I was and what I wanted. These people and this experience have helped me move from struggle to strength.

When my divorce was final, I added to my bucket list that I have had since I was a teenager. I committed to myself that when I sold my wedding ring, I would take a girls' trip with my girlfriends, and that is exactly what I did. I let go of that story with Mr. N, sold my ring, and planned an outrageously fun "closure" trip with some of my closest girlfriends. My Strength Tribe, as I like to call them!

I am enough! These three words bring me back to my pink power dream and Sara Jessica Parker screaming to the crowd, "Don't let the opinions of others stop you from being the best you!"

You need to let go of preconceived notions of who you should be, or where you should be at in your life, and learn to love who you are in the moment.

Life is all about experiences, getting your spark back, and regaining control. Without good, honest, and loving people in your life, this isn't possible. This is one of the biggest takeaways I received after working through the *5 Steps*. So, I ask you, who is in your strength?

You see, friend, the real challenge of growth comes when you have the courage and confidence to rise again after you have been knocked down. It takes courage to start over again.

You want it? Now is the time to go all out and get it. It's not going to be easy. If it were, in fact, easy, everybody would do it. But if you're serious, you will go all out. You have to have space for anything to happen. With getting rid of the racket and the chaos in your head, everything and anything will be possible for you!

If you'll do this, I believe dreams that you may have buried will come back. Every stumbling block you encountered will be transformed into a stepping stone. You're going to rise higher, accomplish your goals, and become everything you were created to be. You will begin moving from struggle to strength.

No matter how long it's been, no matter how impossible it looks, I'm asking you to start and to keep going. The true mark of a champion is one who keeps moving forward despite the circumstances. You keep looking for new opportunities. You keep dreaming. You're in control here. You have the ability to tell yourself, "I am not going to let this get me down. I'm not going to let this destroy me. I'm coming back and I'll be stronger and better because of it."

Take full responsibility for your life. Accept where you are and the responsibility that you're going to take yourself where you want to go. You can decide that I am going to live each day as if it were my last. Live your life with passion. With drive. Decide that you're going to push yourself.

The last chapter to your life has not been written yet, and whatever happened yesterday doesn't matter. What matters is what you plan to do today. Don't talk about it anymore. Make it a reality!

Be patient, trust yourself, and allow these steps to work for you. I believe this is where most people have difficulty. They worry or give up too quickly. The key is to enjoy the journey and not focus on the end result. You do this by focusing on feeling good each day. Believe in *your greatness*!

Simply saying *I am enough* is not going to have any significant impact on your life. You need to *feel* it. It's about embodying what you're saying. It's a hard thing to describe, but you want to physiologically get your mind and body to truly believe it when you say *I am enough*!

Write it with lip stick on your mirror, put it on a sticky note, or tattoo it on your body. Do whatever you need to do! As I mentioned before, I chose the latter option, and forever inked these words on my collar bone. Remember that your thoughts create your reality! So practice this affirmation daily, or whatever affirmation truly speaks to your heart, to effortlessly tap into your subconscious. Soon you'll feel the powerful effects of reprogramming your mind for success.

You are enough. *I* am enough. *We* are enough. Just as we are, in whatever season we're in. And the more we *celebrate* that and *focus* on that, the more *liberated* we become.

I'm praying this over my life and your life today, my friend, because we don't have time to waste in believing anything else! My hope and prayers are that for anyone who finds themselves in times of struggle, that they are able to come to the realization and acceptance that no matter what happens in life, they are *enough*!

Dear Past,
Thank you for all the lessons.

Dear Future,
I am ready.

Journal Page

For your final journal exercise, take some time to reflect back on all that you have learned in this book. What are your biggest takeaways? What goals have you set for yourself? What are you going to do *today* to make those goals and dreams you have for yourself come true?

_____

_____

_____

_____

_____

_____

_____

_____

_____

_____

_____

_____

_____

_____

_____

_____

_____

_____

_____

_____

After a while I looked in the mirror and realized …
after all those hurts, scars and bruises,
after all those trials,
I REALLY made it through. I did it.
I survived that which was supposed to kill me.
So I straightened my crown and walked away like a boss.

With Gratitude

To my parents Ron and Judi Tieri: "Thank you" seems very small to say when I think about all the sacrifices you have made for me. It wasn't always easy—and mistakes were made—but the love you have always had for me has allowed me to forget the past and focus on creating the best relationship with you both. You both have always been my greatest cheerleaders, my biggest fans. You have both been there for me in the most heartbreaking times. Your hugs have always been my favorite. Mom, I know you aren't able to read this book, but I sure hope I make you both proud. All my love forever.

To my Gram: When I lost you a piece of my heart was taken. I miss you every single day. Thank you for being a role model and a woman of faith. Your heart and love for others is something that has left such an imprint on my life. I strive daily to be the woman you encouraged me to always be. The colors of the book cover are in your honor, as I know lavender was your favorite. I love you and miss you more than words can say.

To my TRIBE: MargE Bhola, Kendra Bondie, Rebecca Grabill, Theresa Lewis, Jacquelyn Loerop, Brook Spezia and Rachel VanHorn. There aren't enough words to express my gratitude and love for each one of you. You all have been there when I was at my lowest and you've never given up on me. I am so incredibly grateful for the unconditional love you have shown me, and I will never take it for granted. Thank you for loving me. Thank you for supporting me. Thank you for believing in me. Thank you for being on this journey with me. Thank you for being my strength! I love you!

To my Juice Plus + family and Team Strength: I was looking for a community during one of the lowest points in my life. Then I found this amazing company, and began creating relationships with like-minded, inspiring, and motivated people. This is when my life began to change. Thank you to my mentors, sidelines, uplines, and my team members for showing me what is possible. Thank you for impacting my life during the most difficult of times and for encouraging me to be the leader I know I am meant to be. #healthylivingrevolution #teamstrength

To Nitara Lee Osbourne—my editor and friend: We met unexpectedly and I couldn't wait to get to know you more. Your story is powerful and inspiring. There is no one else I would have wanted to edit this book. Thank you for your encouragement and dedication to ensure that my book turned out exactly how I wanted it to be.

To Sean Douglas, TEDx Speaker and Founder of The Success Corps: First, thank you for your service to our country. I am proud to be your "sister in arms." Go Air Force! Thank you so much for going out of your way to help make this book a reality. Keep changing the world!

To Jessica Medina, author of *Just Travel*: I never would have started this book if it wasn't for your awesome coaching! Thank you so much for all the support and encouragement.

To my Lord and Savior Jesus Christ: Thank you for this life you have given me and for lessons you have taught me. Thank you for the struggles because they taught me to draw closer to you. Thank you for all the amazing people you have put into my life during this journey and for continuing to show me your grace and love. I would be nothing without you.

Appendix

Step 1 Resources

Values Exercise

Your values represent what's important to you in life. Knowing your values helps you understand what drives you, what you enjoy, what inspires you, and what you'd like more of.

By building a life and lifestyle around your values, you create a life that is satisfying and meaningful to you.

Important: values change over time, and deepen as you understand yourself better. They are always moving. Your values can also be situational. For example, what's true for you at work, may not be true for you at home.

Finally, the Sample Values List below is *only* meant to provide ideas. We are each unique, so there will undoubtedly be words that are missing from this list and different words that sum up your values better. Feel free to amend or add to the words in the following list.

1. Accomplishment	34. Focus	67. Presence
2. Accuracy	35. Forgiveness	68. Productivity
3. Acknowledgement	36. Freedom	69. Recognition
4. Adventure	37. Friendship	70. Respect
5. Authenticity	38. Fun	71. Resourcefulness
6. Balance	39. Generosity	72. Romance
7. Beauty	40. Gentleness	73. Safety
8. Boldness	41. Growth	74. Self-Esteem
9. Calm	42. Happiness	75. Service
10. Challenge	43. Harmony	76. Simplicity
11. Collaboration	44. Health	77. Spaciousness
12. Community	45. Helpfulness	78. Spirituality
13. Compassion	46. Honesty	79. Spontaneity
14. Comradeship	47. Honour	80. Strength
15. Confidence	48. Humour	81. Tact
16. Connectedness	49. Idealism	82. Thankfulness
17. Contentment	50. Independence	83. Tolerance
18. Contribution	51. Innovation	84. Tradition
19. Cooperation	52. Integrity	85. Trust
20. Courage	53. Intuition	86. Understanding
21. Creativity	54. Joy	87. Unity
22. Curiosity	55. Kindness	88. Vitality
23. Determination	56. Learning	89. Wisdom
24. Directness	57. Listening	90. _____
25. Discovery	58. Love	91. _____
26. Ease	59. Loyalty	92. _____
27. Effortlessness	60. Optimism	93. _____
28. Empowerment	61. Orderliness	94. _____
29. Enthusiasm	62. Participation	95. _____
30. Environment	63. Partnership	96. _____
31. Excellence	64. Passion	97. _____
32. Fairness	65. Patience	98. _____
33. Flexibility	66. Peace	99. _____

Step 2 Resources

Creating Your Vision Board

Your vision board should focus on how you want to feel, not just on things that you want. Don't get me wrong, it's great to include the material stuff too. However, the more your board focuses on how you want to feel, the more it will come to life.

There is only one major rule to creating a vision board that works, and it's that there aren't any rules. You aren't going to mess it up. You can create your vision board on your own terms. Here are the answers to the most common questions my clients ask:

Q: What should I put on my vision board?

A: Anything that inspires and motivates you. First, think about what your goals are in the following areas: relationships, career and finances, home, travel, personal growth (including spirituality, social life, education), and health. You don't have to cover each area in the same way; just take a mental inventory of what you want each of those areas to look like, and write them down. Always handwrite your goals instead of typing them. There's something energetic about actually handwriting your goals. From your goals and aspirations, think about what you want on your vision board. As I said before, what you focus on expands. You'll be amazed at how things just move forward once you set the intention for what you want and how you want to feel.

Q: Should I have one main vision board, or a bunch of small ones for different areas of my life?

A: It's totally up to you. What makes the most sense in your life? I personally like to have one central vision board that I look at every day in my home office. I have a few small ones that I've made at retreats that I keep around too. Each area of your life affects each other, so starting with one central vision board usually makes sense. Theme boards that center on specific events or areas of your life are great too. For instance, a wedding-day-specific board will help you focus on how you want to feel on your big day. A career-specific board placed within the space on your desk can help you work towards that promotion.

Q: How often should I re-do my vision board?
A: Whenever it feels right. I often leave blank space on my vision board so I can accept new things as they appear in my life. I also add and rearrange images during the year when I feel inspired to do so. Additionally, each December I give the board a total refresh to get clear about what I want in the New Year. Some things stay. Some have served their purpose, and don't make the cut. Go with your instinct, and revise, re-do, or rearrange your vision board when you feel it's time.

What you'll need:

1. Any kind of board. If you're new, maybe start with a cork board or poster board from the hardware store. They run about a dollar. If you can, I recommend a pin board or something pretty you like to look at. I got my 24"x24" white wood framed pin board on Etsy.

2. Scissors, tape, pins, and/or a glue-stick to put your board together.

3. If you want, fun markers, stickers, or anything else you can think of to deck out your board. I don't use that stuff, but if embellishments make you feel great, then go for it.

4. Magazines that you can cut images and quotes from.

5. Most importantly, include the stuff you want to look at every day. Photos, quotes, sayings, or images of places you want to go; reminders of events, places, or people; postcards from friends; or just about anything that will inspire you.

6. Time. Give yourself a stress-free hour or two to put your board together. If you're a social butterfly, invite your friends over, and make a party out of it. I host a vision board party every year on the first night of my partner mastermind weekend. I can't even tell you how much it sets the tone for the event. Everyone is more focused and less stressed after we do it.

How to do it:
Set the mood. Turn off the TV. Turn on some relaxing music. Light a candle and clear your space.

When it comes to actually putting your stuff on the board, I like to leave space in between each item because clutter clouds my mind. I like space. However, if you love the feeling of closeness and want everything to touch and overlap, then huddle it all together and overlap your objects. As for choosing what makes the final cut, lay everything out before you start gluing and pinning so you can get an idea of where you want everything.

What do you think? Will you create a vision board if you don't have one already? I hope the answer is yes.

Step 4 Resources

Morning Power Questions
Answer these questions every morning in your mind or in your journal. Visualize your answer and focus on how you feel!

1. What am I *happy* about in my life right now?
   » What about that makes me happy?
   » How does that make me feel?

2. What am I *excited* about in my life right now?
   » What about that makes me excited?
   » How does that make me feel?

3. What am I *proud* about in my life right now?
   » What about that makes me proud?
   » How does that make me feel?

4. What am I *grateful* for in my life right now?
   » What about that makes me grateful?
   » How does that make me feel?

5. What am I *enjoying* in my life right now?
   » What about that do I enjoy?
   » How does that make me feel?

6. What am I *committed* to in my life right now?
   » What about that makes me committed?
   » How does that make me feel?

7. Who do I *love in my life*? Who loves me?
   » What about that makes me feel loved or loving?
   » How does that make me feel?

8. How can I make myself *feel good* today?
   » How can I improve my relationships today?
   » How can I be present in the now?
   » How can I have more inner peace today?
   » What can I give today?

9. What are *my 5 most important goals*?
   » What can I do today to achieve my goals?
   » What help or guidance can I ask for today?

10. What can I pray for today?
    » If this were the last day of my life how would I live it?

Evening Power Questions

1. What have I given today? In what ways have I been a giver today?

2. What did I learn today? How was my energy vibration today? How can I improve?

3. Did I follow my intuition today and what did it tell me?

4. How did I follow my heart's desires? How did I follow my passion today?

5. Did I allow things to flow today without trying to control the outcome?

6. How has today added to the quality of my life? Am I enjoying the journey?

7. What is the best thing that happened to me today? How can I create a similar experience?

8. Where did I make progress in my life today? Did I celebrate every step of my progress?

9. What am I grateful for today? How did I love today?

Additional Resources

Need some additional guidance to help you visualize your passion and purpose?

Please visit my website at www.missionstrengthsd.com for free downloads of resources to help you, including a gratitude journal, meditation guides, Top 100 Positive Affirmations, mindset workbook, and so much more!

Bibliography

Mandy Hale, *The Single Woman*, 2018.

Tejpal and Dr. Carrol McLaughlin, *Manifest Moment to Moment*, 2014.

Brian Tracy, BrianTracy.com, 2018.

Katherine Hurst, The Law of Attraction.com; *5 Creative Visualization Exercises to Help you Find Health, Love, and Success*, 2018.

Merriam-Webster Dictionary, "Narcissist", 2018

Bonnie Marcus, Frobes.com: *5 Danger Signs That Complacency Will Derail Your Career*, 2013

About the Author

Megan R. Fenyoe, LCSW
Transformational Mindset Coach

Megan R. Fenyoe is a Veteran, Licensed Clinical Social Worker (LCSW), Transformational Mindset Coach, Best Selling Author, Professional Speaker and host of the Blonde Bombshell Podcast. She is a contributing writer for Thrive Global and also owns her own health food franchise through the Juice Plus + Company.

As a Transformational Mindset Coach, Megan will transform your negative self-talk into positive self-empowerment believing you are ENOUGH! How does she do this? She takes you through her proven 5 Step System that will move you from struggle to strength.

Through coaching, leadership, consulting and speaking engagements, she has helped hundreds of people accurately assess their challenges and identify ways they can change, capitalizing on the strengths they already have while building new ones.

WHATS DIFFERENT: Megan has gone through many struggles throughout her life and was living a life without meaning, purpose and just going through the motions. She has successfully transformed every area of her life using her proven 5 Step System and is now living a vibrant beautiful life. A life where she truly believes she is ENOUGH.

Megan's passion and purpose in life is to share her story in hopes to support and encourage others to begin to believe they are ENOUGH.

Megan has been featured on SiriusXM Radio, TV/Radio Shows, multiple podcasts, as well as various magazines. You can find out more about Megan and get a host of *free* tools online at: www.meganfenyoe.com

You can also follow her on social media:

Facebook: https://www.facebook.com/meganfenyoe
Instagram: https://www.instagram.com/megan.fenyoe
LinkedIn: https://www.linkedin.com/in/meganfenyoe/
Twitter: https://twitter.com/meganfenyoe
Podcast: https://www.theblondebombshellpodcast.com

Book Me as a Speaker

Want to interview Megan or invite her to speak for your event?

If you are a member of the press, an event planner and/or looking to book a speaker please contact Megan via email megan@misisonstrengthsd.com or call 858-480-5216.

All of Megan's talks are best as a keynote or a 60-minute presentation. However, Megan can shorten them for 30-minute presentations as needed. Megan always gives high-content, high-value presentations that are energetic, motivating and fun for all audiences.

Megan has a style of teaching and speaking that makes it easy for anyone to follow along, be inspired by and take away more than enough implementable strategies to make substantial shifts in their life. Megan's passion and purpose in life is to inspire others to live healthier. Mind. Body. Soul.

Megan has been featured on SiriusXM Radio, TV/Radio Shows, multiple podcasts, as well as various magazines. You can find out more about Megan and get a host of *free* tools online at: www.meganfenyoe.com/speaking

Made in the USA
San Bernardino, CA
17 December 2018